Contents

Anyone Can Be An Expert Skier 2

Powder, Bumps, and Carving

Harald R. Harb

Anyone Can Be An Expert Skier 2–Powder, Bumps and Carving
A Getfitnow.com Book

Hatherleigh Press/Getfitnow.com Books
5-22 46th Avenue, Suite 200
Long Island City, NY 11101
Toll Free 1-800-528-2550
Visit our Web sites getfitnow.com and hatherleighpress.com

DISCLAIMER:
Before beginning any exercise and recreational skiing program, consult your physician. The author and the publisher disclaim any liability, personal or professional, resulting from the application or misapplication of any of the information in this publication. Skiing is an inherently dangerous sport. You should not depend solely on information gleaned from this book or any other for your skiing safety. This is not a substitute for personal instruction in skiing. Your use of this book indicates your assumption of the risk of skiing and is an acknowledgement of your own sole responsibility for your skiing safety.

Anyone Can Be An Expert Skier books are available for bulk purchase, special promotions and premiums. For more information on reselling and special purchase opportunities, please call us at 1-800-528-2550 and ask for the Special Sales Manager.

LIBRARY OF CONGRESS CATALOGING AND PUBLICATION DATA TO COME
ISBN: 1-57826-178-3

Interior Layout and Design, Photomontages, and Illustrations by Diana Rogers

Cover Design by Peter Gunther

Photos by Byron Hetzler

10 9 8 7 6 5
Printed in Canada on acid-free paper.

About the Author

Harald Harb is president of Harb Ski Systems. An Austrian by birth, he moved to Eastern Canada shortly thereafter. He followed his desire to become a skier from an early age, winning his first regional race in the Laurentain Mountains of Quebec at eight. Harald raced in his first World Cup race at 18 with the Canadian National Ski Team and later was the Overall Pro Ski Champion on the US Eastern Regional Circuit. He then started to coach racers and became a director of racing programs. Harald's understanding of skiing movement developed through study of anatomy and kinesiology, as well as his coaching experience. Harald directed and coached programs that produced some of the USA's most successful National Team members and Olympic medalists. He has been a master coach in the USSCA organization since 1985. He was the program director for Glacier Creek Academy in Alaska, the program that developed Tommy Moe, Olympic gold medalist.

After coaching for 20 years, Harald spent four years on the US National Demonstration Team. He was a Rocky Mt. PSIA Examiner and Trainer. Working with recreational skiers, he was convinced that current teaching systems needed improvement. Harald developed and established the Alignment Performance center concept at Aspen and Telluride. Now he operates his own centers. Harald created the Primary Movements Teaching System™ and the Harb Skier Alignment System™ so that skiers could learn movements and choose equipment to become expert quickly. He is the author of four books on skiing and skiing-related subjects. Over 100,000 lessons have been taught with his system. PMTS Direct Parallel, as it is called, currently is the only teaching system in use that makes a clean break from the traditional wedge, wedge christie progressions.

Harald also writes for *Skiing* magazine and several skiing Web sites. Harald and Robert Hintermeister, Ph. D., co-author of the *PMTS Instructor Manual*, presented the PMTS Direct Parallel System and Harb Skier Alignment System to the 2nd International Congress of Skiing and Science in St. Christoph, Austria, in January 2000. The Association of PMTS Direct Parallel Instructors is a new not-for-profit organization formed for the further education of ski instructors worldwide. Harald is the Technical Director of the PMTS Instructor Association.

You can keep up to date with Harald and Harb Ski Systems on the Web site,

www.harbskisystems.com

Acknowledgments

I just come up with the ideas, ski for the photographs and write the thing, then pass it on to the editors. Presto, that's all it takes for a new book. I only wish it were that easy. This book has been in the works for the past three years. It was conceived right after the first *Anyone can be an Expert Skier*. The ideas came from developing skiers of all kinds. I started with racers. Racers need to learn to ski just like anyone else and they need to learn to ski well before they can ski fast. Too many racers ski poorly and stagnate during their racing careers. I see it all the time at the start of races: coaches and racers rubbing and brushing expensive wax to gain that extra tenth of a second. I watch them ski the first few gates where they lose two seconds because of poor technique. The wax isn't the problem. As long as they are having fun, that's okay, but with a half a day of good ski instruction they could make up tenfold what they try to gain with waxing.

I thank the racers whom I coached over the years; I learned from them as they learned. I learned what worked and what didn't. I've coached 12- and 13-year-old kids who achieved more then I ever dreamed. Some grew up to compete in the National Championships, NCAA, Olympics and World Championships, and some won medals.

I'd also like to thank the skiers who bought my first book and attend my camps and private lessons. I have watched them exceed their expectations, becoming expert skiers in all conditions. They are dedicated skiers and they have drive. They believe in themselves, they know they can do it, but for some reason had never found the answers. These are the skiers who motivated me to develop the ideas for this book. I thank you for giving me the opportunity to work with your skiing, and I thank you for trusting me.

Encouragement and having people believe in what you are doing is as important as personal drive and perseverance. PMTS is developing a huge following. Its not because thousands of people are skiing with me or with the best PMTS instructors, it's because they are reading my books and the methods work.

My greatest supporter as well as critic is my partner, Diana Rogers. Diana is an aerospace engineer, and just as importantly, she is a great skier and coach. I don't know anyone better. She is a graduate of the University of Colorado and has a master's degree from Stanford. Skiers love to ski with her and learn from her. There is no one I know who wouldn't learn and benefit from her coaching. She is so clear and easy to understand. Diana is a deserving member of the small but elite PMTS Training, Teaching and Skiing Team. She takes rocket science and turns it into cooking soup, simple and easy. Diana is also the master of book layout, photo organizing and montage construction. This is her third book and she gets better with each one.

Bob Hintermeister is a friend and colleague. He holds a Ph.D. in Biomechanics as well as an accreditation in PMTS. These credentials make him a valuable instructor and PMTS trainer. Bob is a rock, so solid in his understanding of mechanics and the human body that I feel relaxed and confident with our programs because of his scrutiny. Bob accompanied me to Austria last winter to present PMTS to the International Congress on Skiing and Science. It was one of the highlights of my coaching career. The most prominent scientists and researchers from universities all over the world attended to present skiing research and learn the latest innovations. To that group we introduced PMTS with overwhelming acceptance. Bob is a respected member of this highly regarded academic group. The respectability that PMTS is developing in the scientific community is due largely to Bob's help in developing the system.

Bob Emery is a friend and PMTS instructor and trainer. PMTS, Harb Ski Systems and this book would not be here if it weren't for Bob's dedication and belief in the system. Bob is an attorney, has his own legal practice and is a professor of law. His guidance has been invaluable in shaping, mentoring and guiding our efforts. Bob is the president of The Association of PMTS Direct Parallel Instructors.

Rich Messer is a skiing icon and has been a friend for over 30 years. He has a degree in education and began his official skiing career as the technical director at Stratton Mountain, where I met him. He was a PSIA examiner in the Eastern Division and former Ski School Director at Glen Ellen, Vermont, before it became Sugarbush. Rich has certified in three different national teaching systems and is a trainer and examiner in three systems. He currently is a trainer and examiner for the Association of PMTS Direct Parallel Instructors. He is the ski school director at Silver Creek, Colorado, and builder of the paper bale house, in Fraser, Colorado. Rich is one of the best skiing evaluators I know. He never misses a detail about skiing movements or teaching methodology. He has been a contributor to PMTS and our books since the beginning.

Kim Peterson holds an MA and is currently completing his dissertation for his Ph.D. in education. He is a PMTS trainer and consultant, and is a co-author of the *PMTS Instructor Manual*. He has been of invaluable assistance with editing and content for this book. Kim introduced me to his methods of Student Directed Ski Instruction when I was training director at Winter Park ski school. I immediately enrolled Kim as a trainer in the ski school and we have worked together ever since.

Craig McNeil, friend and ski buddy, black level PMTS instructor and ski writer for the *Rocky Mountain News*. Craig has been writing the only ski information fit to print for the last six years. John Clendenin is former two-time world freestyle champion, PMTS black level instructor and advisor. Thanks to Descente for providing Harb Ski Systems with its uniforms.

There are hundreds of instructors and skiers who have supported us and lent a helping hand through this process of developing PMTS and this most recent book. I acknowledge them here for what they have done for skiing and ski teaching.

Still more thanks to…

Scott Fortner and Loveland Ski Area for the great powder and overall skiing and for providing the locations for photos in this book.

Byron Hetzler, our skiing photographer, for all the great photos.

Mary and Rod Rogers, for their help with editing the book.

Andrew Flach, president of Hatherleigh Press, for his assistance with producing our books.

Foreword

The fact that you have this book in your hands (and are reading the foreword) suggests that you are a serious student of skiing. Even if this is only your second book on skiing (supposing that *Anyone Can Be An Expert Skier* was your first), you may recognize that you are holding a powerful tool. This book does not skirt the issues of physics or ignore the impact of anatomical concerns. Instead, it will guide you right through them.

Skiing has oft been labeled as a simple sport. Many teachers of skiing appeal to the minimization of complex ideas, the simplification of intricate concepts and the reduction of various unrelated notions by retorting, "Keep It Simple, Stupid (KISS)." While this axiom may prove useful to limit jargon or to focus the ramblings of careless instructors, it certainly does not minimize, simplify or reduce the laws of physics. Truly, the anatomy of a skier does not change because someone teaching skiing wants learning to be easy. Similarly, the laws of physics don't change because a skier struggles to understand them.

During the course of reading this book, you can expect to understand more about the common elements of skiing. You can expect to identify movements and patterns that are common to all skiers in all conditions. After reading this book, you can expect to be able to apply those movements to any skiing terrain, under any snow condition, at any time. Truly, this book defines how to become a versatile skier by introducing new vocabulary and innovative exercises.

Harald's vast experience and genuine concern with the issues of skiing have qualified him to identify movements that mediate the successful negotiation of "any time, anywhere" skiing. You may already know that these are called the "primary movements of skiing." The foundation of PMTS is in the "P." Primary means just that: the foundation or basis from which everything else proceeds. Movements that are primary on your first day are also primary on your best day, your most exciting day and your breakthrough day.

Learning to ski has been plagued with clichés. By definition, a cliché is an overused (hackneyed) phrase. Some of these clichés have ceased to communicate any sort of serious meaning. Consider what is meant by the phrase "point your skis in the direction you want to travel." Any instructor of first-day skiers knows that many first-timers possess the uncanny ability to point their wedge across the hill while picking up speed sliding down the hill. How about the suggestion that as you increase pressure on your downhill ski, your skis will come together? It is clear that some skiers' bodies don't allow that to happen.

Exercises can become cliché also. How many "bicycle turns" does it take to become an expert skier? How many steps are really in "thousand steps" turns? While these exercises can produce good movements in some skiers, they are obviously not the answer to every skier's needs. In fact, these overused skiing exercises have become nothing more than calisthenics. No wonder that many skiers are tired of exercises. Jumping jacks were never that exciting either. You will find that the exercises presented here target specific outcomes and produce observable changes in your skiing.

This book represents years of experience, careful analysis, multiple iterations, and volumes of feedback. The descriptions contained herein promise to be concise and accurate. You will discover that these descriptions are reliable. Not only will you understand the descriptions, you will be able to share them with your friends and those who try to describe skiing to you. Skiers finally have a common language that communicates accurate meaning and is applicable across all situations. As you might expect, these descriptions are not always simple…but they are always accurate.

In addition to the vocabulary of expert skiing, Harald has developed the exercises that produce primary movements. Like the words, the exercises are also not always easy. These exercises identify the components of primary movements and provide a way to make the movements habitual. Mastering the exercises will increase your ability to recall the movement any time and anywhere. This versatility is a coveted ability and distinguishes the expert from the recreational skier. The exercises contained in this book would cost hundreds of dollars to accumulate from intermittent ski lessons. You have them now at your fingertips.

Versatility increases freedom. Can you imagine an airplane that is able to fly only in fair weather? What if an airplane were capable of beautiful take-offs but had little capacity to land? Surely, you'd never board those planes. Some skiers pick and choose the runs and conditions to ski based on a limited ability to comfortably ski any time or anywhere. Maybe you've noticed that you shy away from some terrain or some snow conditions. Once mastered, the vocabulary and movements described in this book will increase your freedom. Imagine standing above the run that has always intimidated you, knowing that when you need to, you'll be able to turn, absorb, create balance, or stop. This kind of confidence can be learned only through accurate descriptions and relevant exercises. Now you can ski the hill instead of having the hill ski you.

The "T" in PMTS is also significant. Primary movements can't be communicated in secondary or tertiary generalities. The precision and accuracy of primary movements demand precision and accuracy in the delivery system. For this reason, an experiential approach has been adopted to form the Teaching System for Primary Movements. As you discover primary movements you also access past experiences by creating situations in which you can discover new meaning. By combining new vocabulary with new experiences, your ability to recall those experiences also will increase.

The forces involved in skiing haven't changed; the body parts involved in skiing haven't changed. Since these things have been common from the first pioneers who sought to slide on snow, some ski teachers have concluded that the Primary Movements Teaching System is another description of what skiers have always done. These naïve criticisms resemble the conclusion that since skiing and fishing both use poles, they must be the same. While neither the parts of the body or the laws of physics have changed, your understanding and application of those principles makes you unique in the skiing world. Interestingly enough, many of these "assimilators" who are anxious to reduce PMTS to a reiteration of old ideas were vehemently opposed to PMTS just months ago. We have to salute the dexterity with which ski philosophers adopt, generalize, and accommodate the things they can't mimic or copy. The vocabulary, exercises, precision, and accuracy described in this book distinguish it from previous skiing fads. Like the width of collars, size of pant cuffs, vogue colors and hairstyles, the trendy descriptions of skiing come and go and come again. Like the fact that pants will always have two legs and collars will always be somewhere around the neck, primary movements are reliable, accurate and dependable.

Some teachers of skiing have attempted to disbelieve the success and importance of primary movements. Their disbelief didn't change the force of gravity, the role of velocity, or the impact of friction. The shape of the earth didn't change because Columbus's peers didn't believe it was round. Beliefs and belief systems belong in the realms of philosophy and religion. Ski preachers who promote a system based on belief assume the right to require some sort of charismatic commitment to emotions that can change from skier to skier and from situation to situation. Beliefs influence motivation but don't reduce the importance of movements.

Gravity, momentum, inertia and velocity combined with muscles, ligaments and bones create a common ground for describing skiing. These realities don't change because of beliefs or opinions. The science of skiing is the same today and tomorrow. While the descriptions of skiing vary and the preachers of skiing beliefs impose their charisma on innocent listeners, the realities stay the same. In the end, we have to conclude: it **is** rocket science.

Kim Peterson
October 2000

Chapter 1:

Better Technique, Faster Learning

Shaped Skis Open the Door to The New Way to Ski

The opportunity to improve your skiing immediately has been available for the last four years. PMTS Direct Parallel is providing marvelous, innovative approaches to help skiers improve more quickly and easily. Simply put, by learning PMTS Direct Parallel, you gain a biomechanical advantage.

In my first book, *Anyone Can be an Expert Skier*, I showed how this new method is applied with shaped skis, progressing from the beginning skier to the expert level. Readers of that book responded enthusiastically. Here are some of the typical comments I received:

- "I learned to ski better and improved faster reading your book than from any ski lesson."
- "As soon as I tried your 'Phantom Move' my skiing improved."
- "This is the only technique that should be taught."
- "I am a beginner. Where do I take lessons in your system?"

This book expands on the use of the PMTS methods for advanced skiers and intermediate skiers who want to move up to expert level in all conditions. I show the techniques that I use in my skiing and have developed for the PMTS system. At age 51, I feel I am skiing better than at any time of my life. With the assistance of this new technology, all skiers now have the potential to improve their skiing, as age no longer should be a limitation. Even prior injuries or poor technique need not be obstacles to skiing improvement.

All skiers deserve to ski in a way that produces exhilaration and satisfaction from gliding over the snow. New shaped skis can help make this happen, but most skiers won't achieve their full potential without using the PMTS Direct Parallel methods. Obviously, because short skis are easier to turn than long ones, they will seem easier to use regardless of technique, but you will find that you can have a greater experience by using them correctly. Advanced skiing, such as bump skiing at the black level, requires quick reactions and short turns. And quick reactions require the use of small muscles and low resistance. Efficient skiing requires less effort and fewer muscles. Making it easier to turn, control and direct the skis with small movements is the biomechanical advantage offered by the new ski technology. If skiers have always skied correctly, they will require only fine-tuning and a little experience to be completely at home with shaped skis. My father is 80 years old and has skied since he was seven. He is a certified Austrian ski instructor who started on shaped skis four years ago and loved them immediately in all conditions. He has always skied by focusing on his feet, and in the last four years he has gone further by incorporating the ski tipping actions of PMTS Direct Parallel. Yes, he made minor adjustments to his skiing, but he also noticed that the skis were more forgiving, required less effort and reduced the strain on his knees.

However, skiers using traditional skiing techniques may gain no benefits from shaped ski technology. These are skiers who have developed skiing movements that use big muscles and large body parts as a result of receiving incorrect instruction or learning by surviving. In skiing, overworking occurs when fighting terrain or resisting gravity. Moving big objects or resisting large forces requires large muscle use.

Traditional Skiing Methods

The instructions from traditional teaching systems that engage the large muscles include

- Rotary movements: steering, turning, or rotating the feet or legs to turn the skis
- Timed and coordinated up movements or extensions of the body during turn transition
- Emphasis on turning the outside or downhill ski

All the traditional systems currently in use around the world are based on the snowplow, or wedge, and are biomechanically similar, whether French, Austrian or American. Even systems that are marketed to make skiers believe they are immediately on their way to parallel skiing, for example, the "Fast Track Parallel," are still snowplow-based. The snowplow movement progression imposes clear and long lasting biomechanical disadvantages on a skier's technique.

These methods teach skiers to apply muscular force to redirect the ski they are standing on. This means twisting, steering and skidding the outside or downhill ski. Successfully turning the ski by twisting causes it to rotate, torque the knee and start to skid out from under the body. The twisting and steering causes the ski to become unstable. Survival instincts tell a skier to stand on a consistent, secure platform, so the skier fights to stay over a ski that is moving away and to the side, displaced and skidding. As it continues to skid, the skier fights harder to stay over it, caught in an eternal trap. The easiest way to get out, to escape, is to **stop steering and twisting** and **start tipping, tilting or inclining** your skis.

PMTS Method

PMTS breaks with this tradition, using different mechanics, and setting new standards. Balance acquisition and free foot movements are the basic components of PMTS.

PMTS teaches skiers to balance on one ski and move the other. There are distinct and separate roles for the stance foot and ski and the other (free) foot and ski. The stance foot is the stable, balancing side, allowing the skier to develop confidence. The free foot and ski create the movements to make turns. Applying the combination of **tipping, tilting or inclining** to the inside ski is called the **Phantom Move**. When properly performed, it is smooth, progressive, and barely detectable, hence its name. Balancing over the stance foot and using the free foot to engage the stance ski will cause the skis to arc across the snow. Shaped skis turn virtually by themselves using the Phantom Move. The stance leg remains stable. I started this section of the book by stating that skiing has become easy; what could be simpler or easier than the Phantom Move?

The techniques that skiers learn from the basic PMTS Direct Parallel system give them access to the full advantages of the ski's design by using a series of easy movements that are more efficient, giving the skier a "biomechanical advantage." This is the reason for the amazing success of the PMTS Direct Parallel system.

I am not saying that skiers have never had access to ski design before PMTS was developed. Isolated components of PMTS have been around for some time, but only as fragmented, unrelated snippets, not as a streamlined, complete system. The very best skiers use PMTS movements when they ski. Since PMTS espouses efficient movements and the best instructors teach efficient movements, it makes sense that the most expert and effective instructors have used parts of PMTS.

Some skiers I work with tell me that their instructors use certain aspects of PMTS. Although it may be a well-intentioned effort to jump-start traditional teaching, using some parts of the PMTS system is only a partial solution. Since the basic movements developed by traditional teaching systems cause problems in long-term skiing development, it isn't sufficient simply to "spruce them up" with PMTS components. For many skiers, adding a PMTS movement may yield an initial benefit, yet inefficiencies will still plague their technique. It is my job to reverse these encumbrances by introducing the complete use of PMTS Direct Parallel.

The PMTS method was developed in an effort to make skiing simpler and more effective. When viewed in its entirety, the fundamentals of PMTS are unrelated to other teaching systems. PMTS is based on a simple sequence of moves related to each part of a turn (beginning, middle and end), which provides marked, immediate improvement. In addition, it is easier to understand and to learn because PMTS omits most of the complicated, widely held tenets of traditional ski teaching. (Those who are interested in the theory and logic of PMTS should read the *PMTS Instruction Manual*.)

It has been said that simple solutions are best. That is certainly true for PMTS! Now that PMTS has been used in over 100,000 lessons, skiers and instructors who use it agree that it works faster to produce successful skiers. They ski more easily, experience less fatigue and have more fun.

> *"When I started teaching PMTS, I immediately noticed more rapid improvement and instant breakthroughs for my students, and huge advances for the instructors in my program."*
>
> *John Clendenin*
> *Two-time World Freestyle Champion, director of the Aspen Ski & Board Doctors*

Expert Learning Theory

Most skiers have a history of traditional instruction, so I have applied innovative learning theories to make acquisition of PMTS movements rapid for all skiers. Our skiing clients arrive with a vast assortment of movement concepts that are based on traditional instruction. These tips are a virtual hodgepodge they have accumulated from ski instruction — a little from every "bag of tricks" instructors carry with them. It is obvious students don't dream up this string of often contradictory movements by themselves.

It isn't necessary to travel far to determine the source of these lessons. The instructions can be heard when riding a lift over practice slopes in some of the best ski resorts in the USA. A phrase like "up and around" is a common instructional cue repeated in traditional ski schools. It seems to be the accepted practice: instructors shout these commands to students, reinforcing debilitating movement patterns.

By contrast, as you are introduced to PMTS, you will discover functional information.

Analysis

When I watch skiers, I do a quick inventory check of their movements. Using PMTS, it requires only two turns for the trained eye to see what I call "limiting movements." I mentioned most of them earlier in the section on traditional skiing methods. Once you have learned the basic PMTS movements and know the order in which they are performed, you quickly will be able to see what other skiers are doing on the slopes. In fact, one of the most surprising things about my students is their ability to analyze skiers. I don't train them to notice the limiting movements of skiers. But limiting movements are glaringly obvious; they stand out. I even have had students tell me they see the deficiencies in the skiing of their previous instructors. Once these limiting movements are identified and replaced with PMTS techniques, you will experience a ride you never expected.

Learning New Techniques: RAM and the Hard Drive

There are two levels of consciousness that exercise control over movement: the conscious and the subconscious. Let's explore briefly how these two levels of consciousness interact as you learn new patterns of movement.

The conscious state is the one in which you can introduce new movements and direct control over your actions. When you begin to ski, your conscious mind loads what you want to work on – a new movement, perhaps. Your old technique, ingrained in your subconscious, resides immediately below your conscious mind. In situations in which you stop concentrating on new movements, or when you become apprehensive or unsure, the conscious mind stops controlling movements, and the old information in your subconscious immediately takes over control of your movements.

The conscious mind is like RAM (computer shorthand for random access memory or, as I like to call it, on-screen memory) in a computer. I refer to working in the conscious as working in RAM because it is fleeting and stores little information. If your new movements reside only in RAM, or the conscious mind, they will go away when you cease concentrating on them. They are not yet written on the hard drive.

The subconscious mind is like the hard drive. Once material is written there, it can be reaccessed even if the RAM is wiped clean (perhaps by fear of a steep mogul run). The subconscious is a storage area for the movements and reactions you have learned over a lifetime and use without conscious thought. Your mind automatically applies movements from the hard drive in times of emergency, or when you are fearful or unsure. In these situations, the information loaded from the hard drive takes over; the new material in RAM is wiped away.

Learning new movements is a matter of writing material from the conscious mind onto the subconscious. Until you overwrite the old material on the hard drive, it will return any time you are unable to focus consciously on technique.

The first step when learning new techniques is focusing the conscious mind on concise, effective movements and practicing them. It is the successful repetition of these new movements that causes the body to start recording them in the subconscious, or hard drive. By writing over the old information, new movements are substituted for the old. Once acquired, these movements can be accessed from the conscious mind by beginning the movement. The speed of acquisition depends on the complexity of the moves. Simple, logical, effective moves are learned faster than complicated, confusing, or extensive ones. In other words, the material you are working with in RAM must be in small bits, repeatable and simple.

Fooling the System

Even when we understand how new movements are acquired, it can be difficult to write new dependable information to the hard drive. Anyone who has ever taken lessons probably has experienced this situation. You are doing very well; you seem to be learning new movements. Then the instructor takes you to a slope where you have always had trouble, and you immediately freeze up and revert to what you were doing before the lesson. This reaction is normal. The information from the hard drive is used. The new techniques you have been learning have not replaced them yet, because the body doesn't trust them yet. New movements have to be repeated successfully until the body believes in them and records or writes them to the subconscious or hard drive.

There is a way to open the pathway to your hard drive and allow it to accept new information more readily. The method is called "movement reinforcement" and it is supported by the use of "external cues." Changing deeply rooted movements lodged in the subconscious requires practice with trustworthy information. Learning with the concise, easily replicated patterns used by PMTS creates that trust. PMTS is designed to accelerate the acquisition of new movements using external cues.

External Cues

An external cue is a physical attribute that can be recognized, identified and even measured. To help skiers acquire efficient movements, PMTS relies on actions that focus on outside or external cues, such as the position of the skis or the boots. These cues will help you become more aware of your actions and will allow you to change or remove any ingrained movements easily. The cue can be visual or physical, but it should always be verifiable by observation. An example would be "lift the whole ski from the snow." The external cue is the ski completely away from the snow. You can look at the ski, or you can sense that the ski is no longer dragging on the snow. An added, or subsequent cue, could be "touch the tip of the ski in the snow" or even more specifically, "tilt the ski until the outside part of the ski tip is in contact with the snow." External teaching cues include references to parts of the ski, such as the tail, edge, inside edge, or outside edge. Action verbs presented with verifiable, external outcomes are also effective external cues. The examples used above are good: lift the ski, touch the tip and tip the ski.

Conversely, internal cues are related to body position, movement of the body, or location of parts of the body. Some examples are such classic statements as "hands forward," "bend the knees and ankles," or "move or point the knee out." Success in these instances is subjective and not easily verified or replicated. It's difficult to know how far to move the body part in these examples, and whether the attempt at moving created a desirable outcome. It is even more difficult to repeat the move exactly so that the result can eventually be written to the subconscious.

PMTS was developed as a predominantly external cue movement system. On snow, presentations of primary movements are described by actions and outcomes that can be verified visually, such as "stand on one ski, lift the other ski and tilt it to the little toe edge." Students are encouraged to glance down at their skis to see what they're doing, but not to pay much attention to the position of the body or certain parts of the body. This maintains the external focus or attention on the resulting action itself.

Mastering Movement

It is fair to ask whether there really is such a big difference in the rate at which people learn with external cues, as opposed to internal cues. I've found there are virtually no internal cues that are better than action words or cues to external objects. Even small differences, such as "pull the inside foot back," rather than "pull the inside ski back," are important to note. Although many may find that the foot is synonymous with the ski, others seem to do better if the focus is on the ski rather than the foot.

I don't honestly know whether such a subtle difference will have an actual impact on the learning or success rate. I am familiar with several studies that seem to show significant improvement in learning rates using external cues. Researchers who have performed multiple studies on external cue learning believe quite strongly in eliminating any internal reference if an external one can be used. It's exactly that approach that produced striking variations in performance on a ski simulator studied by Wulf et al (1997, 1998). They focused on the feet (internal) as compared to the wheels of the apparatus, just below the feet (external), and found large differences in learning. There is also a study done by Dr. David Bacharach et al (2000) from St. Cloud University that revealed similar results in performance.

To knowledgeable people, it may sound like splitting hairs to say that movement instructions with well defined outcomes, such as "invert the foot" or "articulate the ankle" should not be used because they are internal cues. However, in dealing with students, I've found that such cues can cause the focus of attention to shift in the wrong direction — away from the resulting action. Using the example of inverting the foot, a preferable instruction would be "show the base of the ski to the other boot" or "dip the tip into the snow," although the difference seems trivial. We should be aware that when discussing technique or theory with someone it is important to understand the internal workings of the body. In this case you don't always have to have an external focus, but when teaching, the material and content should be focused externally.

Now think back to your traditional lessons. Were they focused on internal or external cues? Here are examples of teaching that I've heard or read from traditional systems: "move your hips forward," "use more leg rotation," and the best one yet, "change edges by simultaneously turning your legs."

These are strong examples of internal cues, which typify traditional teaching systems. Compare these with the external cues of the PMTS method.

Learning is Fun

Since repetition is a natural and necessary part of movement learning, learning new movements always should be fun. When new movements quickly improve your skiing, your fun is increased and so is your motivation.

Intricacies of Understanding

Most of us learn new movements successfully if the presentation is

1. something we want to learn.
2. easy to understand.
3. realistically achievable.

Although you may be highly motivated to learn skiing, you easily can become more or less motivated during the learning process. Few of us will go blindly where we have never gone without some insight into the process. Even if you are totally confident that the instructor is "all knowing" and you are ready to do anything he or she wants, there is still an opportunity to increase motivation.

How to Increase Your Motivation:

1. Be given an opportunity to discuss your expectations.
2. Establish agreeable, realistic goals.
3. Receive lessons tailored to your expectations.

If you come to a lesson with expectations that are too high for your immediate capabilities and the instructor isn't aware of these expectations, the lesson will seem a failure to you. You may leave frustrated, even if the instructor has given you what he knows to be the correct lesson for your level of skiing.

PMTS Direct Parallel initiated an instructor training and accreditation program in April 1998. Instructors who are accredited in PMTS Direct Parallel are trained and tested to use methods that evaluate the student's goals and expectations on an ongoing basis during a lesson. This method is called "Student Directed Ski Instruction" and was first introduced by Kim Peterson. Since then, with Kim's guidance, PMTS has developed an accreditation program that focuses primarily on the teaching abilities of instructors. PMTS instructors are unique in the field of ski instruction, because they are the first to be trained and accredited in "Student Directed Ski Instruction."

Fulfillment of Expressed Expectation

In order to set reasonable expectations for yourself, you have to be able to evaluate your own skiing. You should recognize when you are doing something beneficial and know you are doing it successfully. If you have been depending on your instructor to tell you that you are on track or doing something right, then your skiing is not in your control and is dependent on outside confirmation. If you find yourself thinking, "I can't remember whether the instructor told me to turn my uphill ski or my downhill ski," then you aren't evaluating your own skiing. An instructor is useful if he can teach you how to reproduce efficient movement. With PMTS movements it is easy to observe your results and track your progress. When you know what movements to select, and how to generate them with conscious movement cues, you will be able to learn more quickly. With PMTS movements it is easy to observe your results and track your progress. You will also be able to discuss your expectations with your instructor and decide how to work together to achieve them. PMTS instructors are trained to help you become your own best coach.

Become Consistent

As a young ski racer there were days when I was very hot and others when I was not. Some days everything worked beautifully; other days I was lost. This is normal for skiers who don't have a concrete, solid repertoire of skiing movements. This hasn't happened to me since I started to use movements with an external focus that developed balance. I can now produce the same consistent skiing and put myself into my skiing comfort zone on the very first run of the day. I believe every skier can achieve this consistency with the PMTS system of movements and technique.

Let Your Subconscious Take Over

Now that you are accustomed to the idea of controlling your movements by using your conscious mind to give movement cues, I must prepare you to ski without them. When will the right occasion present itself for you to let go? When you race! One of the worst things a racer can do is to think about instruction cues and technique while racing. The conscious focus has to change and turn to selecting terrain, locating turning points and just reacting. Technique is secondary in these situations. An expert skier skis with his eyes and lets the body react to deal with challenges. The mind becomes clear of instructional input and is exclusively fixed on reading terrain and sending that information back to the brain. It is obvious that the brain has to know what to do with the information once it arrives. This is part of what we will discuss in the application of various approaches to all the mountain disciplines.

A great way to learn to rely on movements imprinted in your subconscious is to take racing lessons. Skiing through gates requires that you react rather than think about how to turn. When you are concerned about where to go, you suddenly forget technique. You respond with movements you have trained and learned. This is the ultimate test of your technique and your learning process. If you have learned valid, effective movements, they will stand the test of the racecourse. If the movements are inadequate, you will have problems negotiating the course. The same can be said for skiing in the bumps, powder and steeps. If you are confident with the movements you have learned, these conditions will require only small adjustments and a little experience to master.

In this introduction we have launched many new ideas about ski teaching and learning. The concepts will be reinforced throughout the book. Since this is a self-guide to PMTS Direct Parallel you may want to review this section at a later time. It will be helpful to understand whether you are skiing from your old "hard drive" or using your new programs. Determine when you are ready to rely on movements you have written to your "hard drive". Have you programmed it properly with new efficient movements? The rest of the instructional portions of the book will refer to the most effective external cues. Try to become familiar with them, and possibly invent your own, as you become aware of what works best for your skiing. Now that we have introduced some learning and self-coaching theory, let's begin the PMTS Direct Parallel Undergraduate Course.

Chapter 2:

Balance

Defining the Role of Balance in Sports

As time management becomes increasingly important in everyone's life, accurate, effective training and instruction methods become essential. After performance goals have been defined, it's important to research the best methods for achieving them. For the sport of skiing, a delicate balance — no pun intended — must be struck between physical preparation and technique. Anyone who aspires to become an expert skier on all black terrain must dedicate some training time to physical conditioning. Precise balancing movements and ability do greatly reduce the need for strength. But skiing repeated runs for half a day or longer on black terrain will be beyond the ability of any skier who has no prior basic endurance training. Still, most of the time that a professional or recreational skier has to devote will be spent on technique, not on physical training. Every sport has its own requirements, and training management becomes critical for the participant. Therefore, it is important to determine what the most pivotal component is for progress and then to pursue it.

Although I have trained athletes for competition in other sports including tennis and bike racing, most of my time and energy has been dedicated to skiing. Are you surprised that I recommend a training program radically different from the traditional approaches? The reason I do is because it achieves results. I have been skiing for almost 49 years and coaching for 27 years, and I have observed a fair number of skiers develop over that time. Some of them are skiers whom I followed and emulated in my youth. Many are now in their 60s and 70s and are skiing very well. In fact, many are skiing better than when they were younger.

Let me explain. Skiers who ski well on black terrain don't have to lift weights, run 20 miles a week or take their bikes on century rides. In the off-season, they may go hiking, fly-fish, play golf or tennis, or work in the garden. There is one thing these people have in common: they all learned to ski using balancing movements, and therefore they ski with minimal muscular and physical effort. If this makes sense, why isn't everyone teaching skiing this way? I can only guess that most instructors haven't been trained to understand the process of creating a "biomechanical advantage," which is achieved only when we are in balance.

Let's look at some current trends. When I read about some of the touted shaped ski carving techniques, I have to shake my head in disbelief. They advocate extreme body positions and a very wide foot position. These are fads and aberrations, and some possibly may be dangerous to joint stability and health. In many cases, these techniques advocate static positions with a locked, unbalanced body. Any position in skiing that adds lateral and rotational loads to the knee and accentuates the knock-kneed position makes the knee vulnerable. In these positions, shifting weight results in an unbalanced two-footed stance. It takes great strength to recover from these positions because they don't use efficient balanced body alignment. The terms "gorilla position" and "hunched" are appropriate names to describe these techniques. They lack finesse and balance refinement and should be avoided by skiers who want to minimize muscle fatigue and joint trauma. These techniques are very limiting, producing one kind of turn not transferable to any other types of skiing.

Ski instruction that produces the results you want has to integrate balance into its program. Balance enables the skier to ski with better control and stability and with less fatigue: in other words, with more fun. This is what most skiers hope to achieve by taking lessons. Some of you may be wondering if traditional teaching systems use balance in their teaching. The answer, unfortunately, is that most don't use it to the extent necessary to move skiers to higher levels rapidly.

So what training should you be getting? I suggest it should be an approach that combines balance and technique. My method is designed to develop balancing skills and offers an appropriate mix of activities that quickly improve skiing ability. In fact, in PMTS, the instructors spend more time teaching balance than technique because the skiing techniques are designed to guide the skier through the balancing activities that are needed in skiing.

The Question of Skiing Balance

What is the particular relationship between skiing and something as fundamental as balance? Balance is basic to efficient movement. When you take skiing lessons, you probably hear the word "balance" used by the instructor at least once a session. You may be told about a "balanced stance" or position. And you probably also are told how to find it by standing near the center of your ski. What does the overused yet rarely defined cliché, "standing near the center of the ski", really mean? Don't the bindings already control where you stand?

Standing in balance means we are able to move freely and in a range to recover. Standing in the middle means we are not predisposed to leaning on the front or back of the ski boot. We are standing between the front and back. When we lean on the back of the boot to stay upright, we are not standing in balance; we are leaning back. To be balanced, we must stand in the middle of the boot confines.

When you take lessons do you work on finding your balancing ability, and are you aware of how to stand? Do you perform exercises that test or refine your balance? Do you learn how to determine whether you are in balance during a turn? If you don't, then you are not skiing in a system that uses balance, and therefore the system isn't efficient. If you can't analyze your ability to balance while moving on skis, how do you know whether lack of balance isn't the biggest factor limiting your progress? You may be skiing with a great deal of apprehension and not understanding why. Without a foundation of balance in your skiing movements, your body may be leaning into the slope without your knowing it. Leaning into the slope reduces control and causes the skis to feel uncontrollable; it's logical, then, to feel apprehensive.

Balance versus Stability

We must clear up one point: balance and stability are not the same thing. Standard ski instruction has neglected balance and accepted a low performance standard — stability — which is achieved by using a wide, evenly weighted, two-footed stance. A wide stance may feel stable at first, and it may prevent you from tipping over, but it doesn't develop the balancing ability required to progress to the expert level. If you've been taught this way, you really never have experienced balance. The irony is that once you start skiing faster and on more difficult terrain using these techniques, you'll find that skiing becomes increasingly difficult and unstable. This adds another reason to be apprehensive.

In fact, skiers never become experts by trying to achieve stability. If you watch experts ski, you see them moving continuously with their skis, always in balance. Their bodies are often far to one side of their skis, which is definitely not a stable position, but they don't tip over. Their stability results from their balancing ability. Unfortunately, balance doesn't develop when a skier strives for stability.

A lack of balancing ability will hold you back. Often when skiers try a new PMTS balance movement they say that they feel as though they're out of balance. I try to reassure them that finding balance can be unnerving at first, particularly if they have experienced standing only in a wide, two-footed stance. If you feel as though you're out of balance as you try these new movements, it means only that you haven't learned the balance needed to perform them yet. Finding and maintaining balance complements the advantages of the shaped ski's design. As you acquire the balancing movements that enable you to access the ski's design, you will be pleased to see your skiing improve and to discover that your potential is unlimited.

Technique, Balance, and the Expert Skier

It's time to take a different look at learning to ski. Developing into a good skier is not well understood. What constitutes good ski technique may, therefore, be even less well understood. In an effort to explain how my approach prepares skiers on-snow and in the off season, I will describe some characteristics of expert skiing.

Skiing at expert levels comes easily with a high degree of innate balancing ability. Balance is the ability to stay in equilibrium, but it's more than that: it's comfort in an unstable world. If you are comfortable, you feel confident and safe. Strength, endurance, and power are secondary requirements for expert skiing. Technique should guide the body through the specific balancing movements needed to learn to ski at a desired level. Traditional techniques limit the development of consistent balance, while PMTS develops balance and allows the body to be comfortable when descending in all mountain environments. Skiing in equilibrium is efficient: it requires less focus on technique and less physical effort.

Learning to Balance

I said that expert skiing requires high levels of innate balancing ability. This is certainly true for skiers competing at the world-class level. Ski racing is a competition of balance. Video clearly demonstrates that the best skiers in the world — World Cup racers — are actually in a balancing competition. The ones who win races are the best ski balancers on the planet in that given race. The racer with the best balance needs to make fewer adjustments and compensations on the way down the racecourse.

Adjustments and compensations reduce speed. Fortunately, those of us who weren't born with a high degree of natural ability can improve balance. In my coaching and skiing career I have concentrated on balance development for both competitive and recreational skiers. The results have convinced me that with proper ski technique and exercises, everyone in reasonable health can raise his or her balancing ability. Wherever you begin with PMTS movements, they will improve your balance and therefore your skiing.

When you learn to ride the stance ski and move the free foot, you are developing your system of moving in balance over the stance ski. When we insist that the free ski be moved to line up with the stance ski, we are creating balancing parameters in your skiing. These are parameters that develop basic elements of efficient ski use with a balanced body. We need to be thorough and accurate about the movements that create balance and those that don't. In PMTS we clearly outline what creates balance and reject the movements that don't. If you deviate slightly from the PMTS prescribed movements, balance is compromised. A movement like steering is a disrupter of balance. Steering, defined and introduced as in traditional methods, causes the learning skier to impart skidding and rotational motion to the body and skis. These both disrupt balance. Anytime there is rotational movement of the upper body, it can cause steering, which overpowers engagement of the ski. An upper leg steering movement that changes ski direction or edging eliminates the platform for balance. As soon as the inside ski is planted and used as the second stance ski during a turn, your body shifts toward that ski and to that side. This shift is a loss of balance. When you are no longer standing balanced on the stance ski, it begins to react undesirably. The first thing you notice is that it wants to go straight. The ski will continue to go straight until you can twist it back to the line you intended. Now you are caught in the "twist it to turn it" techniques. You are no longer using ski design to ski. You are using strength and inefficient movements. Accurate description and demonstration of movements is a strong point of the PMTS system. When inaccurate movements are allowed to creep into the system, the results are diminished. As you develop the PMTS basics like a Phantom Move or drawing the free foot toward the stance ski, you will find balance developing. When you don't use these movements, your standards will lower and the quality of your turns will drop.

The unfortunate state of ski instruction is that traditional systems don't intentionally set balance loss and inefficient movements as their goal, but the basic movement progressions are so disruptive of balance that they leave the skier no choice but to use gross, inefficient movements to survive.

Balance Training

I've been impressed by the large gains in skiing performance that can be achieved by balance training in the off season. Skiers now can save time by focusing on simple exercises, and therefore be ready to take advantage of additional ski lessons. No amount of instruction can improve your skiing if your balancing ability is not equal to the requirements of the new movements your instructor is trying to teach you.

As part of the PMTS program, I recommend many different balance training devices, including the use of a tightrope. I have skiers who have taken this advice seriously and built tightrope installations in their back yards. Chris, one of our clients, is devoted to expert skiing and has seen significant improvement in his technique, which he credits largely to his newfound balancing ability. In addition to using the tightrope cable, he supplements his summer balance training with in-line skating and other exercises.

Another tool that I have found to be very effective for PMTS movements is the Skiers Edge trainer. The machine with its newly designed stance plate allows independent tipping of both feet.

Finally, we use a number of one-footed exercises both to diagnose balance problems and to improve balance. My book *Ski Flex*, co-authored with Paul Frediani, includes numerous dryland warm-up exercises that incorporate balance for skiers. Some of them are described here.

Basic Dryland Tests and Exercises

Block of Wood Test

Fig. 2-1. Block of wood exercises

Fig. a. Stand on a block of wood, a 2" x 4" or, if you are very confident, a 4"x4". Keep the free foot off the floor.
Fig. b. Tap the toe of your free foot behind you as far as you can reach without flexing the stance leg.
Fig. c. Now flex your stance leg and see whether you can reach farther.
Fig. d. Tap the toe as far to the side as you can reach.
Fig. e. Tap as far forward as you can reach.

Have a partner mark the spots you are tapping. Repeat the exercise on the other leg. Do five repetitions on each leg.

Block of Wood Exercises with Rope

Place a rope in a circle connecting your tap points from the previous exercise. Stand on the block and follow the rope outline with your free foot. Do this exercise non-stop, very slowly. Start at the back, move the free foot to the front and retrace the circle following the rope on the way back. Repeat the activity five times.

Fig. 2-2. Block of wood exercises with rope

Fig. a. Stand on the block and reach back with the free foot as far as you can.
Fig. b. Reach back and behind your stance leg.
Fig. c. Reach out to the side.
Fig. d. Reach and follow the rope to the front.
Fig. e. Reach across the front to the side.

Bench Step

With a mini step bench or wooden box, place one foot on the lower step. Without using the leg on the floor, step up to a full extension on the bench.

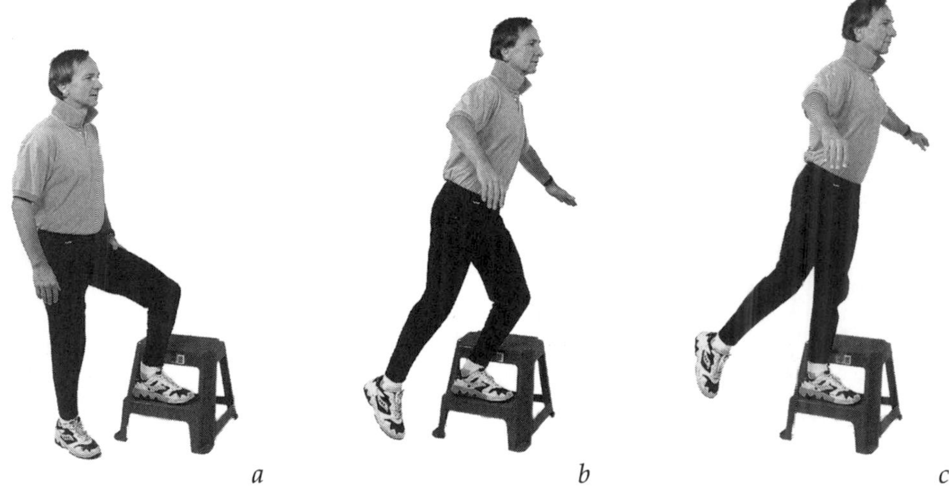

a *b* *c*

Fig. 2-3. Bench step-up and touches

Fig. a. Place on foot on the first step.
Fig. b. Stand up on the step.
Fig. c. Stand up to a full extension.

Front and Back Foot Touches

For an increase in balance and strength training while standing on the first step, tap the toe of the free foot on the floor to the back, side and front of the bench for a circuit as in the previous exercises. Repeat five times.

Increased Difficulty

Place your foot on the top step for increased training difficulty and perform the same routine.

Basic Lunges

a b

Fig. a. Place one foot ahead of the other by a distance of approximately 2 feet.

Fig. b. Flex the front leg until the knee of the back leg touches the floor. Come back up to standing and repeat the exercise 10 times. Change legs and perform the exercise again.

Fig. 2-4. Basic lunges

Advanced Lunges

a b c

Fig. 2-5. Advanced lunges with bench

Fig. a. Stand with your back toe on the bench. The front foot should be about 2 feet from the bench.

Fig. b. Slowly flex the front leg to 90 degrees.

Fig. c. Athletic and well-conditioned skiers may continue flexing until the back knee touches the floor. Do not attempt the full lunge if you have knee problems.

One-Legged Squats

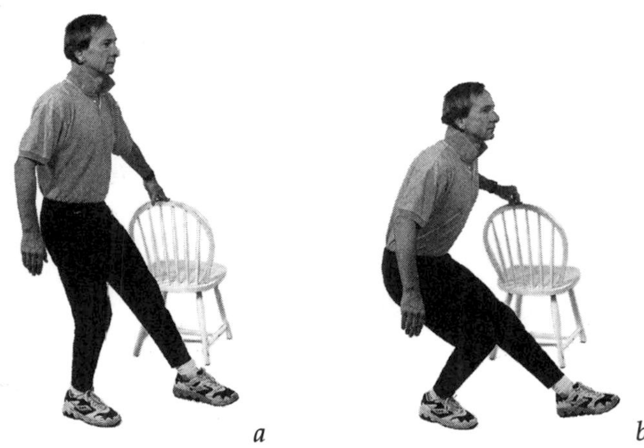

Fig. 2-6. One-legged squats with chair

Using a chair for additional support, squat down on one leg while you keep the other leg a few inches off the ground. Begin with a quarter squat and move up to a 90-degree squat, as shown, after you have developed enough strength. For advanced training do the 90-degree squat without assistance from a chair. Ten repetitions on each leg is an indication of very good leg strength.

Rubber Cord

Fig. 2-7. Rubber cord rear extension

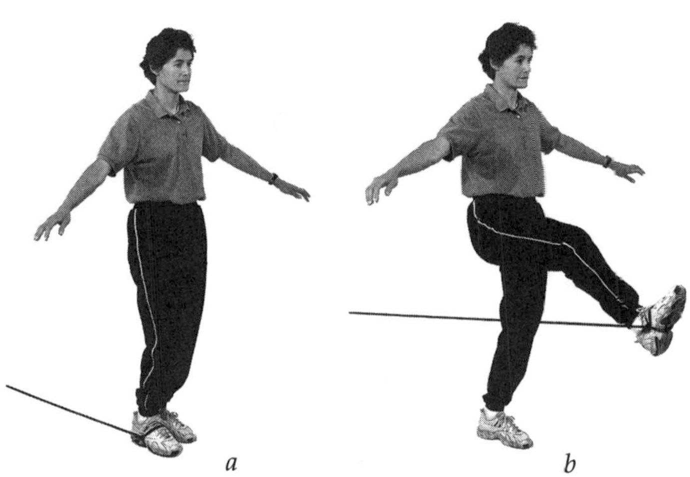

Fig. 2-8. Rubber cord front extension

Attach one end of a sport or surgical cord (found at most health clubs or exercise stores) to a fixed object. Attach the other end to your ankle. Facing the fixed end, move back until the cord is straight on the floor and the ankle with the cord is off the floor. Standing on the stance foot, pull the free foot back until the leg is stretched out behind your body, then return to the starting position. Reverse your position and face away from the fixed end. Move away from the fixed point until the cord is straight. Extend your leg forward until it is straight out in front of your body. Repeat the leg extensions 10 times in each direction for each leg. This exercise provides a triple benefit. It strengthens the leg on which the cord is attached, it utilizes co-contraction of leg muscles like in skiing and it develops balance on the stance leg.

This exercise also can be done to the side. Stand to the side of the fixed point and pull the cord with the free leg away from the fixed point. The resistance for all of these exercises can be regulated by the tension of the cord before you begin the extension.

Tipping Board

The tipping board is a balance awareness and refinement tool. It produces activity in the muscles that balance the ankle joint. Skiers who are not aware of the ankle's influence on balance while skiing may want to build or order a tipping board for balance training. You can find instructions for building a tipping board in the dryland portion of Harb Ski Systems' Web site at **www.harbskisystems.com**.

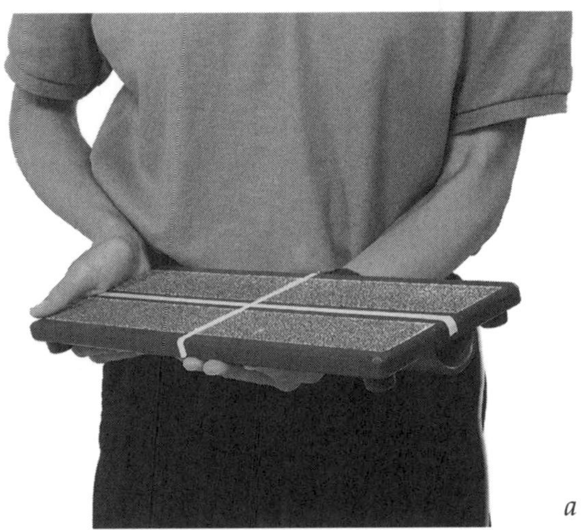

a

b

Fig. 2-7. Tipping board

c

Fig. a. Tipping board.
Fig. b. Using ski poles for added support, stand on the tipping board on one foot and lift the other foot off the ground. Lift the poles off the ground and see how long you can balance.
Fig. c. Center your balance foot on the tipping board.

On-Snow Balance Test: Self Check

How can we be assured we are maximizing our skiing ability? Here are some simple on-snow exercises to test your balance. If you can perform them without difficulty, you are well on your way to becoming an expert skier. If not, there are several ways we can help. A program of the above dryland exercises should definitely help your on-snow performance. If you still have problems, you also may need help with alignment and proper equipment selection. First, try these three tests based on the balanced traverse.

Balanced Traverse

The balanced traverse is nothing more than the basic ability to cross a slope with skis parallel. In the first decades of skiing in the Alps, a traverse was very important because it was sometimes the only way to avoid a steep or difficult slope. Today, at most ski areas, the traverse is rarely used or needed. Turns are connected, and skis are designed so we can easily form round arcs. However, the traverse is still a good way to introduce new movements to skiers as well as a great test of balance. It is incorporated into all Harb Ski Systems' PMTS Direct Parallel lessons. Follow these steps to test your abilities.

Safety Check

Before attempting any of the exercises in this section, you must look in both directions and up the slope. Pick a spot where you can see any skier traffic, and make sure that the slope is clear before moving forward onto the slope.

Criteria

When doing the traverse exercises, try to leave a single thin line with the edge in the snow. The line should be straight. Balance should be maintained the whole way across the slope with the lifted foot off the snow. If you are not able to do it perfectly, do not give up. Practice picking up the lifted ski while standing across the slope; this helps to develop one-foot balance experience. How many skiers have never tried to balance on one foot?

1. Downhill Ski Traverse

Find a spot on an intermediate slope that is clear of traffic. Stand on one side of the slope aimed so you can traverse to the other side. Drop your tips slightly and push off, aiming for a spot on the other side. Make a straight line standing on the big-toe edge of your downhill ski while lifting the uphill ski off of the snow. If you cannot make a straight line across the slope with one ski lifted, you may have an alignment problem. Now turn around and perform the exercise in the other direction on the other foot.

2. Uphill Ski Traverse

This is the same exercise as the downhill ski traverse, except this time you stand on your uphill ski and lift the downhill ski off the snow. Traverse the slope on the uphill ski's little-toe edge. The goal is to scribe a thin, straight line in the snow. Again, turn around and perform the exercise in the opposite direction. The same criteria from above apply here. When you can accomplish this traverse in both directions, you are ready to become an expert skier.

3. Straight Run

On a flat slope with a run out, point your skis straight down the slope. Push off and pick up one ski; hold it off the snow until you have traveled at least 20 feet. Make the skis go straight. Once you have traveled 20 feet, alternate your feet and ski on the other foot for another 20 feet, continuing to keep the line straight.

If you are having trouble balancing on one ski, you may have an alignment problem. No amount of instruction can make a difference in your alignment. First you must align your feet, ankles, boots and skis to the rest of your body before true skiing success can be achieved.

Why Can't You Balance?

When we can balance on one foot, it shows we are able to balance with co-contraction of the lower leg and foot muscles that support the ankle. Co-contraction simply means that opposing muscles are working in cooperation to stabilize the joints.

Co-contraction enables stabilizing movements around a joint to provide fine-tuning and balance. In a ski boot, the range of motion available to the foot and ankle is restricted by stiff plastic. In addition, the shape of the boot determines the angle at which the lower leg exits the boot. If your leg is angled laterally too far to either side, you may not be able to keep your body centered enough to balance on a ski. Proper alignment and a custom-made foot bed can alleviate this situation to a large degree.

Are You Aligned?

Are you suspicious that your skiing isn't right and it's not your fault? Do your friends ski better than you, though you are the better athlete? Have you been struggling at the same level in spite of lessons? Do you feel a difference between one side and the other in your turns? These are the most common situations that have brought the majority of skiers to my alignment sessions.

Evaluate Your Alignment

Proper alignment can change your skiing in one day. It immediately lets you access your balancing ability. I have been developing the process for the last 20 years, and I see the results every day at our alignment center. There are many alignment gurus around — self-professed experts on alignment and boot fitting. If they don't give you a complete on-snow evaluation, they may be missing the most important part of the alignment process. My first book, *Anyone can be an Expert Skier*, has a detailed discussion of alignment, describing what to expect from an alignment clinic, how alignment is improved by the choice of appropriate equipment and the different performance characteristics of various designs of skis and boots.

Equipment and Posture

Skiing is a dynamic and fluid sport. Expert skiing is not the result of assuming certain positions on your skis. It's the product of maintaining balance and using the right movements. However, just as you have a certain posture when you stand in bare feet or in street shoes, your body will have a "skiing posture" as a result of your equipment.

The way you stand on your skis – the posture you display – is to a great extent determined by the geometry of your boots. For each individual, certain brands or models of boots will produce a functional posture. Others will produce a non-functional posture. Ideally, you'd like boots that enable you to

- stand centered on your skis without having to push against the front or back of the boots
- adjust fore/aft pressure on the skis subtly, with small movements of the feet and legs
- recover from losing your balance in either direction.

Ski Boots

In an alignment evaluation we begin with the ski boots because skiers are more likely to receive inappropriate information and advice about boots than about any other piece of equipment. Knowing how your boots will affect your progress is important, because they can have a major positive or negative effect on your balancing ability.

Ski boots are the most influential part of your equipment, the place where the most can go right or wrong. The ski industry — including ski shops, instructors and manufacturers — has demonstrated to me a serious lack of training and understanding in boot selection and fitting through the failure to match boots to skiers. I have numerous skiers who come to my ski camps and alignment centers with the impression that they have had custom boot fitting and alignment done correctly by experts who came highly recommended. During the on-snow skiing assessment, I identify and clients begin to recognize that often they are handicapped by a combination of improper boots, poor foot bed design and misalignment. If you are interested in learning more, the details of how alignment and foot beds need to be measured and made appear in my first book, *Anyone can be an Expert Skier*. Here, I'll describe the influence and limitations of unsuitable boots and how these limitations often lead to incorrect instruction and skiing advice.

You maybe be surprised to know that some of the most popular boots could be the most detrimental to your skiing progress. So then why are they popular, and why do they keep selling? The manufacturers may advertise a lot. The boots might be very comfortable in the ski shop. They may "look good." The ski shop employees recommend them. Professionals who ski on the boots recommend them. Some ski shop employees may have motivations beyond your skiing needs to sell certain boots. It is very easy to end up with the wrong boot for your body type and skiing needs. The shop salesperson doesn't know how you ski, and most traditional instructors receive minimal training about the influence of boots on posture and movement. I said it in my first book: "No ski boot should be sold without an alignment and stance evaluation."

Since the appearance of my first book, in which the characteristics of lateral and rotary boots were discussed in detail, I have received many queries from readers and clients who are anxious to know what kind of boots they should have. Let me briefly summarize the differences in the two types of boots. Lateral and rotary are performance designations that refer to the manner in which a boot transmits edging or tipping efforts from the leg to the ski.

Lateral boots are designed to transfer tipping energy directly to the ski without introducing any pivoting motion. They have stiff sides and a cuff that flexes forward or to the outside. The forward lean angle of the cuff shaft is fairly upright (close to vertical) and the forward flex is controlled to prevent excessive knee drive that causes pivoting on the ball of the foot.

Rotary boots are designed to allow the lower leg to rotate internally before the boot applies lateral tipping forces to the ski. The cuff hinges and rivet positions generally allow the cuff to flex to the inside, letting it move with the legs as they turn and track. Some boots also have significant forward lean, or forward inclination of the shell and cuff. This lean contributes to the transfer of pressure forward to the ball of the foot and therefore produces excess rotation (twisting) of the ski. It causes the ski tail to skid because it becomes light or less engaged. The skier's knee is flexed and the shin rests against the boot tongue. Trying to tip the ski in this position generates strong twisting forces.

One other feature needs to be checked: the boot's ramp angle. This is the angle formed by the heel's being higher than the ball of the foot on the standing surface inside the boot. Ramp angle, when combined with forward lean, can have a profound effect on your fore/aft balance. It also affects your ability to tip the ski on edge, even if the boot has lateral attributes, such as stiff, high sides and a hinge point that allows the cuff to flex straight forward.

Rotary boots may feel great in the ski shop, but once on the slopes they severely hamper your balance and edging ability. Several models from well-known manufacturers cause the most severe skiing performance problems. Don't automatically disregard this explanation because you thought the ski shop salesperson sold you the best product. You may have been told to buy the most popular boots only to find they don't do anything for your skiing. For most skiers, rotary boots are the enemy of high performance expert skiing.

What specifically makes a ski boot rotary? Check all the following factors. Any one may cause your boot to make you lose your edging in skiing.

- If the rivet (that attaches the boot cuff to the lower boot) on the inner or medial side is lower than the one on the outer or lateral side, the cuff can flex to the inside and move with the legs.
- If the forward lean angle of the boot's upper cuff is extreme, uncontrollable, constant loading on the front of the boot may occur.
- If the boot's sole ramp angle is higher than 7 degrees, it may put excess pressure on the front of the foot, leaving the ski tail light and likely to twist out.
- If the boot board is either flat from side to side or has a valgus angle, this will cause excessive pronation. (Forefoot varus and valgus are the amount of twist or torsion of the forefoot, or ball of the foot, relative to the hindfoot, or heel. If the big-toe side of the foot is higher than the little-toe side when the ankle joint is neutral, there is a twist in the foot known as forefoot varus. If the big-

toe side is lower than the little-toe side, the twist is called forefoot valgus.) When the boot board has valgus it means the big-toe side is lower than the little-toe side. Valgus in the boot board causes internal rotation up the kinetic chain. A good foot bed can mitigate this condition.

While any single feature from these examples may not have immediately recognizable effects on certain individuals because of leg length and leg proportions, these are the most common characteristics, either individually or in combination, of boots that are detrimental to skiing performance.

Boot Geometry and Body Posture

Boots come in many different shapes, styles, flexes and geometries. People come in many lengths, shapes and proportions. Different boot geometries will produce different skiing postures for a person of a given build. Some of these postures may be functional, while others are not. It's very important to match the boot's geometry to the individual's in order to produce functional posture. A model of boot that might be perfect for someone 6′2″ with long legs may not work at all for someone 5′6″ with short legs.

A boot with a high ramp and forward lean angles can force you to stand and ski in an overflexed position, with the ankles, knees and hips flexed. This position may put your hips behind center, forcing your thigh muscles to be contracted constantly. This situation is rarely discovered during the excitement of trying on boots. It's only when you go on the hill that you discover your thighs burning and your tails sliding. Tall skiers with long legs are less likely to be adversely affected by boots that have high ramp and forward lean angles, while short skiers rarely ski well with that boot configuration.

Are You Pushing Plastic? *(And I don't mean credit cards!)*

My philosophy about ski boots is simple. You should be able to stand in a boot and not have to flex the plastic when you ski. There is a huge misunderstanding in the ski industry about this subject. Most skiers, instructors and boot shops will tell you that you need to be able to really flex your boot. I disagree.

If you are out of balance in a boot when you stand in it, you have to flex the boot to reach the point where you are balanced, and then it had better be a soft boot because you'll be pushing it constantly while you ski. If you are forced to stand in a less-than-optimal position because of the boot's ramp or forward lean, you will have to flex the boot every time you want to turn. You will have to push forward and flex into the plastic to achieve tip pressure. This effort requires a tremendous amount of work and is not very satisfying. If this is your situation, you will likely not venture too far away from the groomed slopes, as it's a difficult and daunting task to ski in moguls, powder or steeps with this imbalanced posture. Of course, if you are out of balance as you stand in your boots, a stiff boot will make it very difficult for you to ski, as you won't be able to flex the plastic to get to the point where you are centered.

A better solution is to use a boot that puts you in balance in your nominal posture in the boot. In this case, you won't need to push against the boot all the time to find balance. I prefer to select and adjust my boots so that I am in balance between the front or back of the boot. I ski in very stiff boots.

The range of balance in my boots is between the front at the tongue and the back where the back spoiler touches my calf. When I ski, I rarely load the back or the front of my boots unless I get out of balance. If I do get out of balance, I use the stiff front or back to rebound back into a balanced middle between those two spots.

The beauty of a balanced posture in your boots is that small movements are all that you require to make turns. If you are constantly finding yourself in the back seat and working to re-center, it's most likely not your fault, nor is your boot too stiff. I am not advocating stiff boots for every skier. I am advocating a boot that allows you to stand centered and balanced, so that small movements are all you'll need to perform turns. Boot flex shouldn't be softened to make up for an imbalanced stance.

World Cup racers ski in very stiff boots. I find it hilarious when shop sales people talk about Hermann Maier being so strong that he needs a really stiff boot. Hermann Maier has stiff boots because he wants the boot to hold him in fore/aft balance within the extremities of his boot. If he loses balance, the stiff boot can hold him and immediately help return him to a balanced position. The reason he can ski in stiff boots is that he doesn't need to flex the plastic to get balanced; he needs a supportive, stiff boot to regain balance.

The Right Ski Boot

The simplest solution is to buy boots that have ramp angle adjustment and forward lean adjustment. Make sure that the medial rivet on the boot is higher than the lateral rivet.

Foot Beds

Most ski shops try to sell you a foot bed or "comfort insole" with a boot. "Comfort insole" is a euphemism for a $150 piece of plastic to stuff under your foot. A foot bed that will actually make a difference requires a complete process of foot and ankle measurements. (For a detailed explanation, see *Anyone can be an Expert Skier*.) Even foot beds derived from exacting measurements will not produce the correct results unless the technician understands the dynamics of co-contraction. Therefore, a hunk of rigid plastic under your foot won't help your balance. In fact, it may immobilize your foot and ankle to the point where you are required to use large muscles higher up on the leg to balance and make turns — a definite no-no. Old thinking is to lock the lateral movements of the ankle in the ski boot. Our approach at the Harb Alignment Centers is to stabilize the ankle and reduce pronation, but not to lock out the co-contracting ability of any joint.

Co-contraction is not a complicated fancy word used only by biomechanics students. It is one all skiers should know about, because it plays a large role in their skiing success. And it also may help prevent injury. When muscles around joints are acting to stabilize the joint, the joint is protected from exceeding its natural range of motion. The forces of movement are distributed up through the skeleton, forming an "ideal skeletal force line," rather than exceeding the lateral load capabilities of the ligaments. Once you have felt co-contraction and skied using it, you will experience a new sensation: balancing through your skeleton.

PMTS teaches movements that keep your joints stabilized through co-contraction and therefore in balance. External forces are directed through the joint centers and are supported by the skeleton, rather than off-center forces that must be counteracted by ligaments and muscles. Proper alignment and the right boots bring the forces of skiing through and closer to the functionally stacked skeleton for a large majority of skiers.

Skiing Results

Shaped skis, I have repeatedly stated, should make skiing easier and more fun. The reason that skiing on shaped skis is easier is directly attributable to their wider tip and tail. The design allows the ski's tip and tail to cut into the snow when tipped on edge, bending the ski into an arc that creates a turn. The skier benefits because there is less fore/aft balancing adjustment required to make the turn. Shaped skis have eliminated the need to make the big fore/aft body adjustments and tip pressure that were required on traditional skis to engage the ski tip and start a turn.

The coaching in this book rarely mentions leaning forward or pressing forward. Our demonstrators for the book are well-balanced skiers who stand centered over their skis. They ski by standing normally in their boots, and thus balancing on the center of the ski. A proper stance, or balanced posture, distributes pressure as needed to the front and back of the shaped ski. When you are properly positioned and balanced in your boots and you need more tip pressure, you can achieve it with a simple, subtle, easily controlled movement that doesn't disturb your overall balance. PMTS advocates pulling the free ski back to increase tip pressure on the stance ski. The pull-back move is described in two places in the book: Chapter 6, "Free Foot Management"; and Chapter 13, "Bumps."

Instruction

Unfortunately, many skiers don't experience the benefits of shaped skis when they try them. I read and hear that many skiers are still told to press forward or move forward to engage the tips of shaped skis. I find that this motion disrupts balance and is excessive for turn transition. This movement is necessary only when the boot is compromising your position. If you are out of balance to the rear, then you'll need to battle forward to begin each turn. The advice to apply tip or forward pressure is usually circulated by instructors who have a compromised situation in their own skiing, or who find most of their students in a locked, rearward position. Typical instruction to cure this malady focuses on driving your knees and projecting your hips forward. These instructions are ineffective and cause many other problems not related to the fore/aft situation.

Imbalanced posture should be remedied with boot modifications, not by technique. No amount of ski instruction will change your stance. In fact, altering the ramp and forward lean angles of the boots can change your stance quickly. Again, more information on this topic can be found in my first book.

Much ski instruction is a band-aid for a poor equipment set-up. Even a good instructor at times will have to teach you adaptive movements based on your stance and alignment. Adaptive movements don't facilitate your skiing progress; they do allow you to get down the hill better for that lesson. This situation is less-than-acceptable as the next time the snow or the slope changes, the adaptive movements you were taught won't apply. There is real skier stagnation built into this predicament. You are always working on overcoming inappropriate movements and poor balance due to your equipment, alignment or a position that results from that combination.

Performance Check: The Phantom Javelin

Balancing ability should be the defining mark of every expert skier's competence. The path to your skiing success is outlined and presented in a step-by-step program throughout the chapters of the Undergraduate Course. One of the standards is the Phantom Javelin turn. The exercise of practicing and learning the Phantom Javelin is worth the effort as it is not exclusively a test of balancing ability. It also produces functional angles for resisting forces and maintaining balance through natural reaction to the lifted and positioned free ski. If you can perform this exercise as described in the photos, you are ready to move on to the Undergraduate Course. If you cannot perform it at this time in your development, spend extra time working on stance foot balance as you venture into the Undergraduate Course. The Undergraduate Course is a valuable guide to becoming a versatile all-mountain skier, and solid stance foot balance is a prerequisite for success.

Fig. 2-8. The Phantom Javelin turn

Fig. a. As early as possible, lift the inside ski and hold its tip slightly crossed over the tip of the stance ski. Notice here that the ski is lifted into position well before the skis aim down into the fall line.

Fig. b. Hold the lifted ski over the tip of the stance ski while you tip the free foot to the outside, increasing the ski's edge angle.

Fig. c. Keep the inside hand level with the outside hand.

Fig. d. Keep the lifted boot close to the stance boot.

Fig. e. Use no steering or turning. Your outside leg should stay long or straight while the stance ski does all the work. As no leg steering is used and the upper body remains quiet and stable, it's easy to maintain balance on the stance ski.

Fig. f. Ready the pole plant by swinging the tip of the pole forward.

Fig. g. Prepare to set the lifted ski on the snow and to transfer balance to that ski. After the transfer, the previous stance ski becomes the new lifted Phantom Javelin ski. Make sure the ski is lifted and in place during the upper third of the turn.

Undergraduate Course

The Undergraduate Course teaches you the "bulletproof" turn for all-mountain skiing.

If we were to compile a list of the requirements for success in various sports, the composition of this list would be surprisingly consistent. Whether it is skiing, tennis, golf, biking or fly fishing, each has a fundamental set of basic movements that must be mastered before you can enjoy the activity. Acquiring strong fundamentals is a process that requires dedication to details as well as practice. But if there is strong enough motivation to reach the level at which you enjoy the activity, then the time spent developing the basic skills properly will be well worthwhile.

If your only interest in skiing is in being outdoors, then dedication to acquiring precise fundamentals is less critical. However, even if you aren't determined to become technically proficient, there are certain essential skills needed to function in a mountain environment. Establishing control is one of the necessities that requires a certain mastery of technique. So why not learn techniques that not only give you complete control but also lay the foundation for becoming a proficient skier? PMTS Direct Parallel offers both in one package.

If the goal is to experience the thrill that sliding combined with g-force excitement brings, then going well beyond fundamentals is critical. It is no coincidence that the best extreme skiers in the world have years of formal training behind them. Magazines and videos may give the wrong impression of extreme skiing. These skiers are highly trained professionals. This training can come from a number of different skiing backgrounds, such as freestyle, bump competition or racing. Acquiring the fundamentals or basics is a necessary foundation for assuring ongoing growth in any discipline. It can't be done without real dedication.

Consider Tiger Woods. What makes him the greatest golfer of all time? Besides his innate talent, it's in large part his dedication to improving his game. He is already a great and consistent golfer, yet the day before the US Open, he still felt it was important to practice putting for two hours. He did this because he thought his ball wasn't rolling properly. And the night before the last round of the PGA Championship, the manager of the practice range had to ask Tiger to leave, because he was closing the facility for the night. Anyone who applies a fraction of that dedication toward developing proper skiing movements can master the basics for all-mountain skiing. Remember, Tiger didn't wait until he had a chance to win to start applying himself; instead, he is favored to win major titles because he has dedicated himself to his game from day one.

Our culture, in an attempt to make learning more fun, seems to leave out some important words that are integral to success, such as "dedication" and "effort." Because "work" doesn't sound like fun, it is the one word we really avoid mentioning. My point is obvious: if you are willing to dedicate yourself to learning functional, effective techniques, then becoming an expert skier in all-mountain conditions is possible. The information in this book will provide the techniques; from there, the amount of dedication required depends on how expert you want to become.

My frequent discussions with ski instructors have yielded some interesting observations about the need for fundamentals, particularly in relation to those who believe they are ready to learn different forms of off-piste (ungroomed) skiing, as well as to skiers already accustomed to skiing on black, or expert, terrain. The reality is that many of these skiers haven't been introduced to the fundamental requirements needed to handle these situations, even though their dedication is at the right level! What most skiers don't realize is that their training has been based on techniques that get them onto the slopes with an emphasis on control. The use of traditional techniques described in the first chapter creates skiers who use too much power and strength to ski. These are skiers who overuse their joints and muscles to stay in control and who rarely venture into powder and bumps. Such skiers have yet to develop a complete game or to complete the Undergraduate Course. Valid fundamentals needed for all-mountain skiing are rarely incorporated in these traditional progressions, which means that even those who are already skiing on black terrain will acquire new skills and increase their skiing pleasure with PMTS Direct Parallel.

Tennis provides a great analogy. To play tennis, you must first learn to get the ball over the net. Much of your beginner time is spent hitting the ball back and forth, forehand and backhand, but those moves don't make the game. The fundamentals of the real game are rarely learned. Components that make you a tennis player — not just a hitter — such as the serve, volley, half volley, approach shot, movement at the net and overheads, are rarely learned. Tennis novices can be compared to skiers in this sense. They haven't learned the different elements to develop a complete game. To ski bumps, powder and crud, and even to carve, requires a complete game; that is, a command of all the fundamental elements. These fundamentals rarely made an appearance in the lessons you received when you learned to ski. It therefore stands to reason that most skiers are unsuccessful and have great difficulty skiing in off-piste conditions.

Common scenarios for skiers who want an advanced off-piste lesson often unfold in a typical manner. Usually the instructor recognizes a skier's lack of fundamentals at the beginning of a lesson and suggests they spend some time on a groomed slope to smooth out the rough edges. Unless this refresher includes a package of strong "all-mountain tools," it won't further the skier's ability to ski off-piste. A specific course of movements for all-mountain skiing needs to be demonstrated and practiced. Without some clear, basic abilities, all-mountain skiing will not become a reality. The instructor has to know these fundamentals or you will be rehearsing the same movements that you have already learned and which proved inadequate in the first place.

Developing effective, all-mountain techniques can take a very long time if you are coached with traditional methods. No one wants to become an ongoing experiment, learning through trial and error with a coach as the cheerleader. The actual proven skiing skills you need are introduced in this section of the book and can take as little as a few weeks to learn if you follow the program with determination. If you are motivated, you can become an expert in the all-mountain realm. Below is a list of what constitutes the complete game of skiing. It provides you with a self-check to confirm that you have achieved the necessary basics. Evaluate your progress using the book. "To thine own self be true" — and you won't fear or have reason to be concerned in all-mountain conditions.

The Basic Short Turn

This series of photos of advanced, carved short turns demonstrate the complete game. When a skier can ski with these movements, I know we can move on to expert terrain and all-mountain conditions.

Some readers will identify Harrison, my son, from his appearance in my first book at the age of seven. He was 10 when these photos were taken. Many will say he is a natural skier, so of course skiing comes easily to him. I can say this isn't the case. Harrison skis several weekends a season and a week or two with me, but he is not in an organized ski program. He is involved in many sports, including soccer and hockey. He has worked very hard to achieve this level of skiing using PMTS and will tell you that his balancing and free-foot tipping took concentrated effort before they became second nature in all-mountain conditions. If Harrison hadn't learned using these movements, he easily could have fallen into the skidding and rotating methods that hold back skier development.

The Complete Game of Skiing

Fig. a. Harrison establishes complete balance on the stance ski.
Fig. b. In almost exactly the same position as the previous photo, he tips the a free foot further on edge. He has the capability to hold the free foot under his body, as indicated by the ski tail, which is held higher then the tip.
Fig. c. He moves his balance slightly aft by raising the ski tip, but otherwise, the stance ski is making the turn.
Fig. d. He raises the pole tip to prepare for the pole plant.
Fig. e. He relaxes the muscles of his legs to flatten the skis.
Fig. f. Harrison raises the free foot of the next turn so he can begin tilting it toward the outside edge.
Fig. g. Tilting the free ski further to establish firm balance on the stance foot starts the ski carving.
Fig. h. Holding the free foot back under his hips brings more pressure forward to shorten the turn radius.

Harrison demonstrates all of the important abilities that let me know he is ready for all-mountain, double-black diamond slopes. These abilities are

- a clear command of his balance from one turn to the next
- a functional, flowing pole plant with no upper body rotation
- the ability to maintain his skis at the same edge angles
- turns that result from balancing and tipping with no sign of leg steering or twisting
- the ability to control fore/aft balance with his free foot
- hands and arms held in a natural, supportive position to allow freedom of pole swing
- upper- and lower-body coordination.

One additional ability is missing from the list of fundamentals for all-mountain terrain. Can you name it? If you said "leg steering," you will have opportunities to learn a great deal about skiing later in this book. The answer is flexion or leg retraction. Although Harrison didn't need to use it here, he didn't demonstrate any up-unweighting either, so I am confident he will be able to use absorbing or flexing movements to release the ski on steeper bumpy terrain.

The above list of fundamentals in Harrison's "Complete All-Mountain Game" for expert powder, bumps and carving can be divided into three categories:

- Balance Management Protocols
- Upper and Lower Body Coordination
- Foot Use and Ski Edge Angle Awareness

To ski the whole mountain, you'll need a solid short turn. The first chapters of the Undergraduate Course will teach you the basic elements of the short turn — the fundamentals. The later chapters will refine the short turn, and you'll learn how to apply it specifically to ungroomed snow. There is an extensive chapter on coordinating the upper and lower body and using the poles properly, which are essential for skiing off-piste.

It all begins with two fundamentals to help you balance: the "Quick and Easy Changes" of Chapter 3.

Chapter 4, "Releasing," makes sure you start each turn on the right track. It breaks down the exact movements you'll need to start every turn. The release has several variations — all are important to the all-mountain skier. Learning an effective release may make the most difference in your skiing.

Begin by trying the releasing movements in your short turns. Test your balance in short turns by doing a series of connected turns with a very slow release as I demonstrate in the photos. You may find you can't perform the slow release perfectly at first. When you do these exercises slowly, it emphasizes balance and correct movements.

Use the external cues described in each of the exercises. Gradual, progressive flattening of the skis, starting with either the two-footed release or the release from the uphill edge, will determine your success. You are training yourself to control ski-tipping. If you lose control and flatten the ski too quickly, it will grip or lock on an edge and restrict turning. The ski that will redirect to the fall line should remain almost flat through the release until it's in the fall line (pointed straight downhill). At that point it is important to stay balanced on that ski. Balanced in this case means that the other ski is light and tipping to create actions of turning. No turning should be initiated on the stance ski. After the skis complete the turn back across the hill in the other direction (almost to a stop), make sure you are balanced fore/aft, ready to release for the next turn. You may stop after each release at first as you learn to coordinate the movements. Refine the movements of the free foot introduced in these chapters to build on your balance and ski control abilities. After practicing, you'll have better dexterity in using your skis.

After learning an effective release, you'll want to make sure that your movements to complete each turn complement the efficiency of the release. You won't want any "limiting factors" to creep into your technique, make you work harder and hinder your progress. Chapter 5, "The Free Foot

Turns the Stance Ski," will help you learn the low-energy way to ski, getting the most performance from your skis. This technique works in all conditions, from carving deep trenches to zipping through the bumps to floating through powder.

In Chapter 6 you'll refine the actions of the free foot. The free foot controls all aspects of the turn after the release. You'll be able to control the size, shape, and radius of your turn using subtle movements of the free foot.

Most of the chapters in the book include a performance check so you can gauge your progress. If you have trouble achieving the performance standards, you may wonder whether you are doing something wrong. Often, it's not a matter of the wrong movement; it's just a need for a little more practice, or perhaps a refinement of the movements. Use the cues for success to guide your practice. If you are making the movements as prescribed in the chapters you are doing everything in your power.

An example of this very situation occurred last spring at a PMTS Instructor Accreditation course. One of the instructors trying for the Blue Level Accreditation was having difficulty with the bumps. His skis would split apart after a few turns and the downhill ski would jam against the bottom of a bump, tossing him out of rhythm. The condition clearly was being caused by a lack of balancing ability at the point at which the skis headed straight down the slope. The instructor was splitting the skis and using the inside ski as a balance crutch. I took him aside at the top of the next run and asked him whether he was pressing the releasing downhill ski against the new outside ski as soon as the turn began. It was obvious to me that he wasn't pressing enough. He said that he was trying to press the free foot against the stance foot throughout the turn and that by about the middle of the turn, he would lose his balance. I had him stand across the slope on the uphill ski and lift his lower ski. I stood above him. I used my pole to push his downhill ski away from the uphill boot. I asked him to press it back up and keep it in contact with the uphill boot. He pressed and he pressed and finally he was able to bring the boots back together. His comment was, "Is that how hard I have to press to keep my boots together?" I said, " Yes, at least until you feel how it works." The very next series of turns were his best in the bumps. He was astounded that a little thing like pressing harder made all the difference. His trainer who observed him skiing a run later couldn't believe the change in his instructor's skiing. The instructor was successful and achieved his Blue Level.

This example demonstrates how important the small things are in skiing. This breakthrough was not highly technical. It was simply a matter of refining a component in an otherwise effective skier. Take each new chapter or refinement in the Undergraduate Course seriously. The instructor I mentioned is just one person who will swear to the validity of this advice.

The following "troubleshooting guide" will help you to determine what to refine or focus on in order to improve your short turns.

Goal	Exercise or Focus	Benefits
Improve balance	Narrower stance (Chapter 3)	Easier balance transfer
More ski performance	Lighten or lift the releasing ski (Chapter 3)	Immediate transfer, early balance, early engagement of the ski
Connected short turns in balance	Shift balance to stance ski by lightening previous outside ski (Chapter 5)	Balance transfer
Shorter turn	Free-foot refinement, pull the free foot back toward the stance boot and hold it there (Chapter 6)	Increased tip pressure, centers upper body
Maintain corresponding ski edge angles	Flatten lower ski before upper ski (Chapter 4)	Clears lower ski (moves it out of the way) for stance ski to redirect into the turn
	Ball control exercise (Chapter 6)	Proper order of movement; tension between legs keeps legs acting in unison
Ski with less effort	Before turning, pull the free foot in toward the stance boot and tilt it to the outside edge (Chapter 5)	Creates movement of mid-body into the next turn, engaging the skis
Quicker transitions	Relax and flex the stance leg to start the release (Chapter 7)	Let momentum pull your body into the next turn; the quicker the flexion, the quicker the transition
Controlled release	Release from the uphill edge (Chapter 4)	Immediate and balanced direction change, develops edge change versatility
Upper body coordination	Stabilizing pole plant (Chapter 10)	Keeps mid- and upper body stable while you actively tip the skis

Chapter 3:

Toward a Solid Short Turn

A solid short turn is the prerequisite for all-mountain skiing. I notice that most skiers don't have this short turn in their repertoire. Of course, they can make a pushed, skidded short turn, but that's not good enough. You must have at your command a short turn that will stand up to the demands of all-mountain skiing. The short turns used by most advanced intermediates and even some advanced skiers commonly have the following deficiencies:

- pole swing and plant not synchronized with the turn, or a lack of upper and lower body coordination
- turn transitions without a transfer of balance
- skis held at different edge angles to the snow, at turn entry and exit
- outside ski twisted, skidded, and pushed to an edge set
- inside ski constantly trying but failing to catch up with the outside ski to achieve a parallel position.

A short turn is the universal tool for the all-mountain skier. Without it you basically are going into gravitational warfare without weapons. Skiers with an inadequate short turn usually describe it like this: "It's fine on the blue terrain, but when I get on something steep or bumpy, I can't control my speed."

If this description seems at all familiar, take heart, you are on the verge of a breakthrough. The good news is that if treated early and properly, the patient has a long, strong, healthy skiing career ahead. As of now, PMTS has not failed anyone who showed up with these symptoms. Unfortunately, about 90 percent of skiers have these symptoms.

Two Quick and Easy Changes

Through the Undergraduate Course we are going to build a short turn you can rely on and use to advance to the Graduate Course. The Graduate Course introduces you to all-mountain, condition-specific tactics. However, you don't have to wait until graduation to notice improvement in your skiing. If we override a few old habits with one or two simple new movements, an immediate change is at hand.

The first two changes to your skiing will seem almost too simple and easy to be believed. The results are immediate improvements. The changes may contradict what you have been learning and conflict with your present movements and skiing. However, there's no need to be concerned, as the explanations for the changes are given below, and the results speak for themselves. Your satisfaction will be the determining factor; I have no doubt that you will enjoy seeing your skiing efficiency increase. Let's jump right in and start with the wide stance.

First Change: Narrow Your Stance

Here I make a short turn in a relaxed, easy-to-hold stance. The free ski is completely free to tilt or to pull back under my hips. I can switch balance from one foot to the other easily in this stance. If I encounter powder, bumps or crud, I don't need a different technique. This one is completely versatile.

Fig. 3-1. A functional, narrow stance

Fig. a. Lighten the free inside ski and tip it toward its outside, little-toe edge.
Fig. b. Flex the legs to prepare to release.
Fig. c. Maintain both skis at same edge angles.

Cues for Success

- Keep the inside ski light or off the snow to confirm balance on the outside ski.
- Touch the inside boot to the stance boot to learn a narrow stance.

Biomechanical Advantage

- With a narrow stance, your body can move quickly as a result of small adjustments at the feet.

A wide stance is one of the most enfeebling positions in skiing, yet it is taught every day. A wide stance forces you to distribute your weight between both feet. The wide position makes it difficult to shift balance quickly and precisely as needed in bumps and steep powder runs. In bumps, a wide stance will put your skis on completely different levels and pitches, and it may not fit in narrow troughs. In powder, a wide stance generally puts the skis at different edge angles. In the softer snow, this makes the skis converge or diverge quickly and unexpectedly. The results are frequent face plants. A wide stance also forces you to ski mechanically with gross movements of the legs. Now someone will surely ask, "By gross, did he mean 'large' or 'ungainly'?" I mean both. Skiing with your skis and feet apart is ugly and inefficient, requiring large, tiring movements. Almost all skiers who come through our system are comforted to learn that they are permitted and encouraged to ski with their feet in a narrower stance. Say what you like about skiing, most people want to look elegant and ski with style. A wide stance doesn't do anything for your skiing image or the new outfit.

Narrow is Not Glued Together

The kind of narrow stance we are talking about developing is not the locked feet of the wedel technique from the 50s and 60s. The feet should have the flexibility to move independently, but your legs should stay in contact. Separation of the feet (the distance between the boots) is important to achieve, not in width but in the vertical plane. The inside ski boot can be separated from the outside boot but still lined up close to the outside leg. Space between the ankles in a lateral plane should remain narrow (a couple of inches), as in *Figure 3-1*. Note that the amount of vertical distance (one boot is higher then the other) employed in this aggressive turn can be large. My free foot is close to the stance leg but separated vertically from the stance boot. This distance is not only acceptable, it is critical to achieving acute body angles to the snow.

Fig. 3-2. Lateral proximity vs. vertical separation of feet

Second Change: Transfer Balance, Stand on One Foot

Diana demonstrates a clear, clean balance transfer to the new stance foot. She does it by raising only the back of the ski and tilting the whole new free ski and foot to the outside edge. No steering or turning actions are initiated on the stance leg or ski. All the actions at the stance ski are passive, reactions to the initiating actions of the free foot.

Fig. 3-3. A clean transfer of balance

Fig. a. Balance on the outside ski through the previous turn.
Fig. b. Get ready to release by swinging the pole and increase flexion/relaxation of stance leg.
Fig. c. Previous stance leg has released and lifted. Notice how free ski and boot are pulled back and held under body.
Fig. d. Free foot is tipped and held close to establish balance on and engage new stance ski.
Fig. e. Turn is established, balance is solid on the outside ski.

Cues for Success

- Lift the free ski tail just a few inches from the snow.
- In transition, keep the free foot against the stance boot.

Working on lifting one ski and balancing on the other is a simple and quick enhancement to your short turns. Stop standing on two feet! I still can remember during my racing career running in the fog at Whistler Mountain in the National GS Championships. My downhill ski was bouncing like a water ski crossing the boat wake. I was losing precious distance every time the ski bounced. I only realized later that I was never in balance over my ski. Each edge change resulted in too much of my weight being on or over the inside ski, on the uphill side. The outside. lower ski had weight on it, but my balance was never in line with the supposed gripping edge of the lower ski. Once I realized I was making these errors, I made it a priority to build a decisive balance transfer into my skiing. Concentrating on deliberately transferring and establishing balance allowed me to develop a powerful GS turn, even on the toughest, bumpiest runs.

Incorporating these hard-earned lessons, the PMTS system has helped countless students learn more quickly and enjoyably. Teaching one-footed balance right from the beginning instantly makes you a better skier. Understanding and recognizing the feeling of your body balancing over the ski as it cuts the snow is a world apart from the jarring vibration of a bouncing ski, yet few skiers are aware of the difference.

Developing the ability to lift the ski for a particular exercise or in a series of turns is a basic requirement for learning balance in skiing. After you have learned to sense and perform the lift, you will notice how your turns are more stable and balanced. The difference between your new turns and your previous turns is so great that the two no longer will be comparable. Skiing on all surfaces with a newfound ability to transfer and balance, will increase your confidence dramatically. Once you have completely assimilated the balance and transfer technique, the necessity for a strongly lifted ski is reduced. You can and will leave the ski on the snow or lift it when necessary. Lifting the ski is done initially to help you recognize and confirm the transfer of balance and to judge how well you maintain balance through a turn. Quick, connected short turns are learned more easily with a lift to transfer balance. After you are able to identify how much unweighting is needed to balance on the stance ski without completely lifting the free foot, just lightening will be sufficient.

How High Should You Lift?

This exercise doesn't require lifting the ski 12 inches off the snow. One inch is just as effective as one foot, as long as the movement to raise the ski causes a complete transfer of balance to the other ski. As you become familiar with balance and are able to transfer with precise timing, lightening the ski will be sufficient.

Fig. 3-4. Sufficient lifting of free foot

Fig. a. Transfer is complete; slightly lift the back of the free ski.
Fig. b. Pull the heel of the free foot back to hold it under your hips.
Fig. c. Keep the free boot lined up with the stance boot; the tail is still slightly lifted.
Fig. d. The free ski can be placed on the snow but only with light contact.
Fig. e. The tip of the free ski can be lighter than the tail to finish the turn.

d *e*

Cues for Success

- Lift the free ski tail to transfer balance completely to the stance foot.
- Keep boot toes even fore/aft.

Fig. 3-5. Free foot lifted too high

Too High

In *Figure 3-5*, the free ski is lifted too high, which causes too much pressure on the front of the boot and ski, potentially causing the tail of the stance ski to skid. The leg muscles are overworked by lifting and holding the ski so high. This position is tenuous in rough terrain.

The Wide Stance Myth

Remain assured that there are instructors and coaches who will insist that lifting the ski is out of vogue and passé. These are the teachers who have their young racers and students struggling with balance transfer and stability on rough terrain. You may notice that at times the best World Cup skiers ski with both skis on the snow and at other times lift one ski. The reason for this is that they know how to balance and when to lift. They have spent hours training and learning balance transfer. They are able to lift a ski when needed, or leave it on the snow at any given point in the turn. If you can balance on one ski, you'll certainly be able to balance on two; if you know how to stand only on two feet, you won't be able to balance on one. For skiers who have not learned balance on one ski yet, a locked, wide, two-footed stance is their only possible method. The irony here is that when World Cup skiers are on perfectly groomed snow, they can ski in perfect balance and transfer balance perfectly with both skis on the snow. Coaches are so eager to have their racers emulate this that they teach only that position. They believe immediate success is just a matter of widening the stance and keeping both skis weighted or pressured. What they fail to realize is that the World Cup racers have done their homework. They can balance efficiently while skiing in a wider stance. They have learned it through the formal steps that you have begun to use to develop balancing ability. Many developing racers miss the important development stages. Most recreational skiers are stuck in the two-footed, wide stance like many of our young racers.

Chapter 4:

Releasing

The release is the important first action that begins a turn. When we ski in powder or in crud we cannot afford mistakes in technique which is why I have devoted so much effort to developing the release. A correct release sets you up for success through the rest of the turn, while you'll struggle to make up for a poor release. It is important to understand the basic mechanics of the release. I have broken it down in a number of different ways to present examples of how releasing movements can influence your skiing as well as to demonstrate that releasing has applications in all forms of skiing.

The releasing mechanics described here are not a review of *Anyone can be an Expert Skier*. The short turns in this book are more advanced. In the first volume, several chapters are dedicated to the development of the basic release. If you are not familiar with those releases, it would be helpful to review them first. The advanced release described here is developed from those fundamental techniques.

All-mountain skiers must have a solid two-footed release, and preferably a strong ability to perform both an uphill ski and a downhill ski, or weighted, release. Precise control of ski edge angles, often absent when inefficient mechanics are used, is much more critical on variable snow, powder, or bumps than in groomed conditions. The advanced release explanations and exercises will help you learn to keep the skis at the same edge angle from the start to the finish of a turn.

Because one of the goals is to achieve a functional two-footed release, we must learn how to have both skis change edges and maintain the same edge angles to the snow. The beginning Phantom Move, which you encountered in the previous chapter, instructed you to lighten or lift the releasing ski, which can evolve into a two-footed release. The basic movements are the same with only a refinement of the lifting and tipping, making this easy to accomplish with relatively little practice. These types of releases are covered in this section.

Later, in Chapter 8, you'll learn the Weighted Release. After you complete the releases and understand the movements thoroughly, you will learn the "float." At that time you will see how two-footed releasing helps to develop the float, which is so important in powder and crud skiing.

The Two-Footed Release

Prepare Your Boots and Skis Before You Release

From a starting point standing across the slope, focus your concentration on your skis and the rest of the body will take care of itself. The lower ski, or stance ski, will be weighted and gripping the snow. The uphill ski starts out tilted to its uphill, little-toe edge, at the same angle to the snow as the lower ski. You should notice that in this starting position it always requires more effort to move the uphill ski to the same angle as the lower ski to achieve equal angles because external rotator muscles don't have as much tipping, pulling or turning leverage as internal rotators.

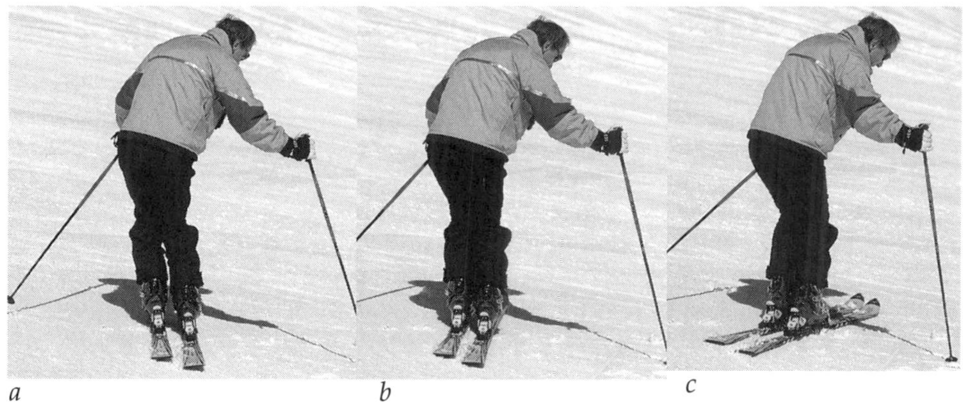

a *b* *c*

Fig. 4-1. The two-footed release: the basic release for short turns

> **Biomechanical Advantage**
>
> • Holding the free foot back, so your boots are even fore/aft, creates a strong turning force on your stance ski.

Fig. a. Start on a blue slope standing across the slope and put the lower pole into the snow for support.

Fig. b. Begin to flatten the lower ski, and let the skis move together.

Fig. c. The tips will begin to fall to the slope. Press the lower ski toward and hold it against the upper ski.

Cues for Success

- Squeeze your feet together as you flatten the downhill ski.
- Pull your free foot back to keep the boot toes even.
- Tip your free ski so its outside edge drags on the snow.

Refinements

There is one common glitch that happens during this exercise: moving the uphill ski to an edge. This is evidenced by the uphill ski flattening before the downhill ski, or by the uphill tail flaring open. If you continually push the uphill ski to an edge before the downhill ski is released to the fall line, begin with the next exercise: "release from the uphill edge". Pushing the uphill ski to an edge indicates that you are not releasing the lower ski.

When the skis reach the fall line, pull the free, inside foot back and tip it strongly to the outside edge. This movement usually requires more tipping action than you have used previously. If the ski is on the snow, slide the foot back and tilt the ski until its outside edge is dragging on the snow.

d

e

f

Fig. d. Use the pole for support and stand on the outside stance ski. The skis will move forward and down slightly.

Fig. e. Notice that I have not moved down the slope, as indicated by the pole, which is still planted in the same spot. Begin to tip the free ski as you hold it to the stance boot.

Fig. f. Keep the free ski back, holding the boot back and lined up with the stance boot. Be prepared to begin a release in the other direction. Use the same set-up as at the beginning of this release by planting the ski pole downhill below the feet.

Debunking the Myth of Simultaneous Edge Change

Traditional teaching systems use the term "simultaneous leg turning," to explain how to move when switching edges and steering the skis from turn to turn. I have to warn skiers that this term is misleading, and implementing it may hinder their progress. The reason so many skiers have difficulty making a strong parallel turn is because they try to steer their legs rather than tip or tilt their skis. Using leg steering movements to make turns results in converging tips and skidded turns. I know this phenomenon well. The focus on simultaneous leg steering in particular causes many skiers to suffer from wedge turn entries, while they actually believe they are making a parallel turn. A true parallel turn always will require sequential movements — but the correct sequential movements, done properly. The confusion and misunderstanding of this issue arises because the movements were described after analyzing photos of expert skiers, rather than from studying biomechanics. I admit that if I focused on describing what the legs were doing in some parts of an expert turn solely from photos, I would have to say the legs turned or rotated. However, what we cannot learn from a photo is whether the leg action is actively creating the turn or passively following from an earlier movement lower in the kinetic chain.

In PMTS, the ski tipping or tilting movements that start at the base of the body — at the feet or skis — do have an effect on parts of the body higher up the chain. When you focus on these movements, you can easily and precisely control the skis' angle and direction. You also are able to put yourself in balance immediately and maintain it. We will see the results of effective movements from the base of the chain in the following example: stand across a slope and move your skis to increase the angle of both skis to the snow. Use the tipping and tilting movements of your feet and ankles to increase and then decrease ski edge angle. If you continue to move the skis to and from a sharp angle, you will notice that your legs rotate toward the slope as the skis increase edge angle and away from the slope when the skis' angle decreases. Your legs follow the angle changes of the skis. We call this *passive, secondary,* or *resultant leg rotation*. Leg rotation may result from tipping the skis, but it should not be a focal point of expert skiing.

Active leg rotation occurs when you intentionally steer or rotate your legs to turn your skis. The large or gross motor muscles of the upper leg must initiate this action. These muscles have little fine-tuning ability to control the skis' direction or edge angle. Therefore, initiating turns with steering and changing ski direction by gross movements such as leg steering, diminish your skiing control and limit your progress.

You will notice that in PMTS Direct Parallel the description of releasing focuses on the outside or downhill ski of the previous turn. To release from a turn, this ski is activated first to initiate a sequence of movements, some separated by only a fraction of a second, which make the transition to a new turn. It is absolutely essential to master them. As the turn progresses, especially if it is a short, aggressive turn, the old outside ski, which becomes the new inside ski, must continue to tilt more actively to its outside edge after the release. This movement is emphasized because it is more difficult to tip a ski to its outside edge than to its inside edge. The muscles on the inside of the leg which control internal rotation have greater mechanical advantage than the external rotators. Because of the way the muscles are connected, in a turn transition, the uphill foot, ankle, leg and ski have an easier time moving to the big-toe edge than the downhill ski has moving to the little-toe edge. The downhill, or new inside, leg must flex and rotate externally under the body. Accomplishing this movement often requires some training. If this release is new to you, focusing on it exclusively at first will provide long-term results.

Release from the Uphill Edge

The release from the little-toe edge of the uphill ski is a skill that all expert skiers must develop if they are to continue improving. Slowly reduce the edge angle of the uphill ski until it begins to slide downhill. The tip drops and the rest of the ski will follow. Hold the free foot and boot close to the stance ski. Press the inside ankle rivets of both boots together to hold tension throughout the turn. If the free foot drops or touches the snow before completion, you have lost balance; start over. Tip the lifted ski strongly toward the outside edge as soon as the your stance ski points downhill. Try to complete the turn within a vertical distance of two ski lengths.

a b c

Fig. 4-2. Release from the uphill edge

Fig. a. Pick up the lower boot and hold it against the upper boot. Do not allow them to separate during any part of this exercise. You may look down to see whether the boots separate.

Fig. b. Start to tip the lifted foot toward its little-toe edge. Use the pole to help you balance as the stance ski rolls from upper, little-toe edge to lower, big-toe edge, as a result of free foot tipping.

Fig. c. Control the rate at which the stance ski rolls to flat – keep it slow.

Fig. d. Continue to press the free boot against the stance boot while you tip it toward the outside edge. Pull back slightly on it to keep the boots even fore/aft.

Fig. e. Notice again how little forward travel is accomplished, yet the skis have changed direction, now pointing downhill. This is achieved not by twisting the ski but by releasing the edge, tipping the free foot and balancing on the stance ski.

Fig. f. The stance boot is blocked from view because the free boot is lined up exactly fore/aft with the stance boot. Holding the boots like this creates turning power. You are accessing your biomechanical advantage.

Biomechanical Advantage

- Lifting the free foot brings a level of balance awareness needed in short, snappy, energetic short turns.

d

e

f

Cues for Success

- Balance on one foot, and keep the free foot lifted throughout.
- Hold your boots together.

Action and Timing for Each Leg

In the transition of the turn, the action of each leg is different. The legs move or rotate in different directions from each other, which is why it is important to begin moving or releasing the lower ski first. If you try to move your legs at the same time, the dominant uphill leg, rotating internally as it rolls from its outside edge to its inside edge, will react more easily and quickly. The "internal rotation response" is already very strong in most skiers. The downhill, or stance, ski must release from a gripping big-toe edge, flatten, and then tilt to its little-toe edge. Because the lateral movements toward the big-toe, or inside, edge require less concentration and happen more readily, they need to be slowed, delayed or controlled. If you try to grip too soon on the new big-toe edge for the next turn, you will force the tail of that ski to flare out and cause a wedge entry to the turn. This is active leg rotation. When we understand this process, we can see that the lower ski needs to tip first, before the upper ski, in order for both skis to maintain the same edge angles during releasing and engaging.

It is difficult for many skiers to learn this new sequence because traditional systems reinforce the opposite movements. If you learned to ski with conventional movements, as most of us did, you learned the snowplow and stem Christie early. As a result, your dominant movement pattern is to move to the big-toe edge by adducting and internally rotating the upper leg, which produces the steering used to turn the ski in the wedge progression. Traditional teaching systems depend on these movements for control and turning.

In the PMTS system, releasing the downhill ski, using the opposing set of muscles, produces turns and creates an external rotation of the stance leg to the little-toe edge, which releases the stance ski and starts the turn.

To become an expert skier, you have to unlearn leg steering and rotating movements, which is why I referred to traditional teaching progressions in my first book and video as techniques that teach skiers dead-end skills. It is frustrating to try to advance to the expert level with these outside-ski steering movements dominating your technique. Few ever achieve expert skiing this way — and those who do usually have improvised and learned on their own.

By using PMTS Direct Parallel, you can reverse these ingrained movement patterns involving leg rotation and learn correct movements. The focus in PMTS is on the external cues of tilting or tipping the skis, which make the legs react in a controllable and predictable manner. Other benefits are improved balance and ski hold, both achieved with less physical effort. When you learn to release using the PMTS way, your center of mass or mid-body moves toward the new turn in a completely different way: deliberately, and under your control.

Two-footed Release from Traverse

Just as you hold your feet and ankles at an angle to maintain your grip while walking on a steep side hill of a golf fairway or a hiking trail, you must grip a snow slope with the edges of your skis and boots. The feet and ankles control gripping actions. Before you start, make sure you are able to hold your skis at the same edge angle while stationary on the slope. Releasing is done with both skis. Stand well centered over your skis and keep your feet directly under your body. Begin by flattening the lower ski first, letting the upper ski follow. Keep the lower or bottom ski weighted as you flatten. Again, this technique is different from the basic release in which the ski was lightened as it was tipped. Avoid the tendency to tip the uphill ski flat faster or sooner than the downhill ski. This caution is the key to avoiding the common problem of digging the big-toe edge of the uphill ski into the snow when releasing.

Fig. 4-3. Two-footed release from traverse

A Different Look at Releasing

Another way to begin this two-footed release is by lessening the edge grip of the lower ski. Press the ski down toward its outside edge. Press or let the outside edge of the ski drop toward the snow. Let the upper ski follow, and then continue moving both feet and ankles together. Be aware that the upper ski will have an easier time releasing, as it is moving toward its big-toe, or inside, edge. As the skis flatten and grip less, they will skid slightly. Make them slide together as one unit, as if the skis were made in one piece like a mono ski. Presenting the skis to the surface at the same angle will make them easier to control and more predictable. It will be easier to stay balanced.

Flattening movements should be progressive – they shouldn't suddenly flatten or roll all at once. See that both skis flatten the same amount. The tips will start moving downhill together. This moment is when skiers have a tendency to lean or sit back on their skis. Instead, keep your feet under your hips and move with the skis as they begin to slide forward and down the mountain. No muscular effort is needed to direct the skis; simply let the tips aim down the mountain. When the skis are pointed directly downhill into the fall line, the release is complete. Both skis should be flat on the snow. Let the skis run; there should be no hurry to twist them into a turn at this point. If it is difficult to feel when the skis are flat on the snow, go to a place on the mountain where you can experiment with a straight run. Take the time to learn what your skis feel like when they are truly flat on the snow.

Skis Flat at the Same Time

In the process of releasing from one set of edges and rolling toward the other, you have no choice but to go through a point where each ski is flat on the snow. Either both skis become flat simultaneously or one is flat before the other. It is very important to be aware of this transition point in a turn. You must be able to determine how your skis are lined up at the transition. In uneven snow or deep, soft snow conditions, both skis should become flat at the same time. Try to keep them flat as long as you can; avoid tipping the outside ski for the turn to its big-toe, or inside, edge. You will achieve parallel skiing with control and balance throughout the turn by managing the new inside ski and allowing the outside ski to come to an edge passively.

Straight Run

Become familiar and comfortable with your skis when they are flat on the snow by skiing this way as often as you can. There are multiple opportunities on a ski run to have your skis flat. Whenever you reach a point on the mountain where you can run straight, do so — especially on cat tracks or on flat sections. Bring your feet together as you try to keep the skis flat on the snow. Find the spot where your skis are completely flat to the snow and hold them there, keeping them flat and parallel. Take a peek down at your skis to make sure they are flat. I can't tell you how many students come to me who are desperate to learn to ski parallel. As soon as we come to a flat area, I have them allow their skis to run straight. Most are amazed when I point out to them that their skis are in a wedge position while they are in the straight run. If you are not aware that your skis are wedging, you will never ski parallel. You may be surprised at how closely together you must hold the skis for them to ride flat on the snow. Many skiers have never become parallel skiers because they have been trained to ski with their feet apart. A wide stance keeps the skis on both inside edges, which means they are not flat, parallel or at the same edge angles. In a straight run, make sure your skis are flat and parallel.

Performance Check

If you can bring your skis flat at the same time for each edge change in transition, you are on your way to skiing success. On flat terrain with no obstacles or skiers around, look down at your skis during edge changes to make sure you are controlling your skis and edges properly. Slow down and watch your skis between turns to see that your skis remain parallel throughout the transition and that they reach flat together as you roll or tip them from the previous edges to their new edges.

Chapter 5:

Tip the Free Foot to Turn the Stance Ski

The first conventional skiing concept we must reverse is the idea that we turn the skis. Skiing by trying to turn your skis is counter-productive. To bring back the pleasure of skiing,

don't turn your skis.

You will learn the key components in PMTS that allow you to make better turns without turning your skis. In this chapter we review the Phantom Move introduced in *Anyone can be an Expert Skier*. In subsequent chapters you'll learn how to relax between turns and give yourself time to achieve balance by using the "float." This new concept will quickly undo the old habits related to turning your skis. The other unfortunate technique, stemming from the lack of PMTS fundamentals that must be reversed is nicknamed the "unibody turn." This requires specific efforts to overcome. I have developed several new approaches that will unlock the body and develop "upper and lower body coordination."

By incorporating the simple changes I proposed in Chapter 3 — narrowing your stance and standing on one foot — you can quickly eliminate two of the most progress-hindering problems in skiing: skidded turns and loss of balance. You may have noticed that it isn't difficult to reverse some of the techniques you were taught and get on your way to becoming a much improved skier. In fact, when we review the Phantom Move, you will be able to eliminate almost all the wrong movements and be on the road to acquiring the right ones.

Analysis of Limiting Factors

Before you can change your skiing, it is important to become aware of the factors that are limiting your progress. The real skill is the ability to differentiate between the actual cause and the visual manifestations of limiting factors. Here is an example: most instructors easily can see when skiers rotate the upper body too much when turning. A logical diagnosis here is that you are compensating for lack of leg steering by employing extreme upper body rotation. Most traditional instructors will tell you to increase leg rotation, or steering, to turn your skis, which in turn should reduce the need for upper body rotation. In addition, they may suggest countering movements of the upper body for you to work on while you increase leg steering.

This solution may seem logical. Perhaps your rotary skills are insufficient. The problem with this approach in actual application is that no increase in leg steering will make you an expert skier. First, it is very difficult to control or sense the degree of leg rotation because this is an internal cue. As discussed earlier, internal cues are ineffective for producing functional movements and results. Second, it is almost impossible to become more active and forceful with leg steering without incurring mid- and upper body rotation — exactly what you are trying to reduce because gross motor muscles are required to move the thighs and trunk. And, finally, steering your skis and rotating your legs to create turns eliminates access to and use of the ski's design — your biomechanical advantage disappears.

The actual limiting factor is the turning of the skis. Here is how I overcome upper body rotation with PMTS Direct Parallel: in the case of the skier described above, there is little or no activity at the base of the body, or base of the kinetic chain, as I call it. The needed movement is tipping the free ski toward its outside edge to engage the side cut of the stance ski, thus using the biomechanical advantage. I begin by introducing new activities that make the student aware of the skis and the angles of the skis to the snow. These cues are external, enabling the skier to judge his or her own performance of the tasks. The object is to substitute new and efficient ski tilting movements for the old forceful leg rotation and steering actions.

There is an important consideration when changing someone's skiing. Even if the technique is incorrect, it is the only way the person is able to ski at the moment. If you are going to take away a movement the skier has relied upon, you must replace it with one that creates a better result. In this example, the skier is rotating the upper body. Only after the student has learned how tipping the skis helps produce a turn will he or she be able to diminish the need for turning the skis by rotating the upper body.

If you are planning to use this book to teach yourself, which I encourage, you are becoming your own instructor. When you are ready to learn a new movement, you must know how to introduce it in a way that makes it easy to learn. To help you succeed, break the movements down into sufficiently small components so that you can build on the exercise.

Let's apply this approach to the case above. The process begins on a flat slope, learning the exercises that create recognition of free foot tipping and stance foot balance. I would start with an introduction to free foot tipping or tilting by describing how to take the downhill ski and roll or tilt it toward the outside edge, flattening it to the snow. This releases the ski from the turn, so a new turn can develop automatically without a deliberate steering force. The focus for the rest of the turn remains on this ski. Next, continue tipping it toward its outside edge until the other ski starts to turn.

This example demonstrates the key ingredients of a successful beginning for a student: easy steps and external cues. The next step is to learn the building blocks that create a balance transfer, which are the basis of the Phantom Move. The Phantom Move, introduced in my first book, has grown in reputation and become legendary thanks to its effectiveness. Lito Tejada-Flores has adopted it in his teachings, and refers to it as "phantom edging."

Fig. 5-1. The Phantom Move

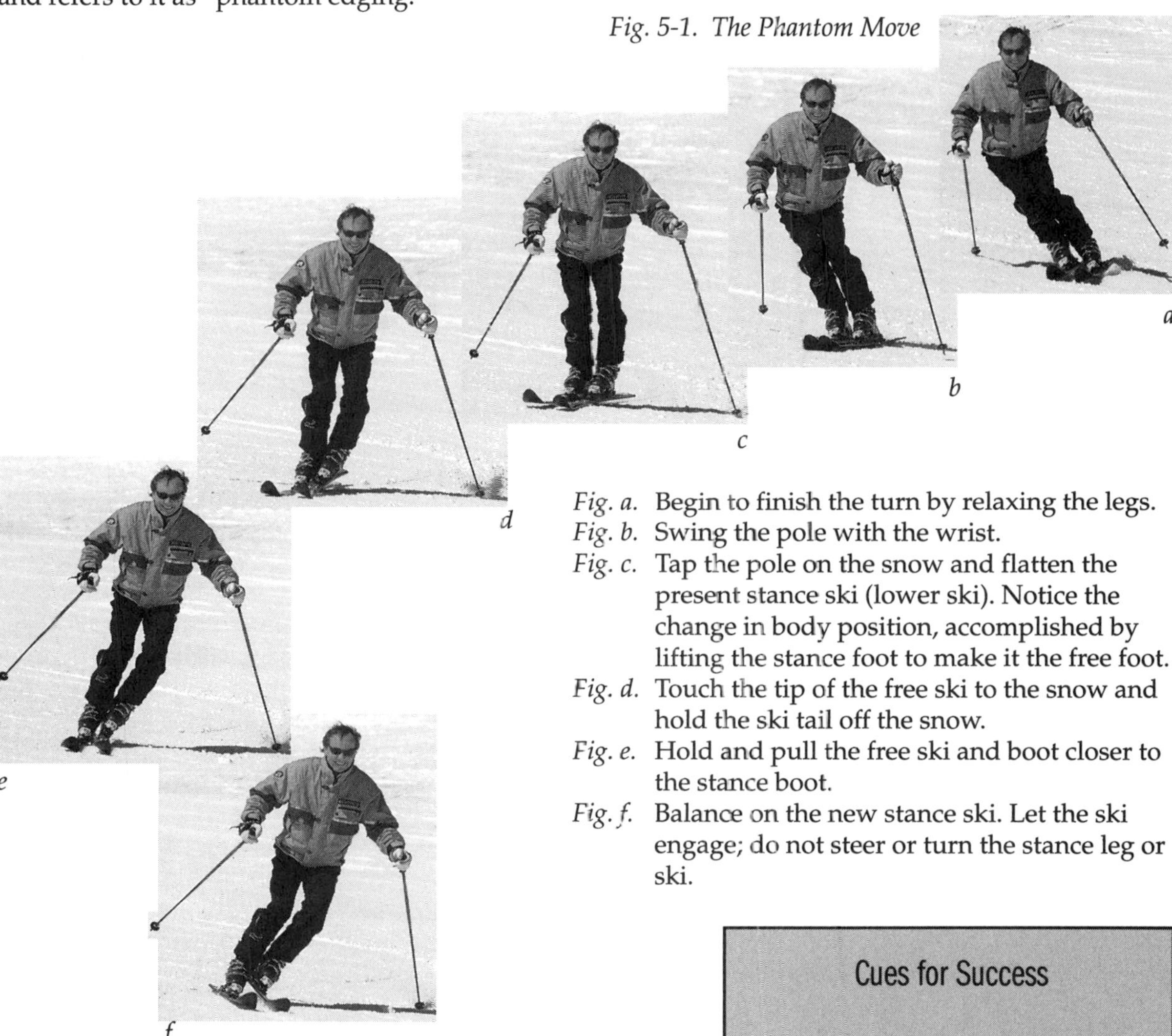

Fig. a. Begin to finish the turn by relaxing the legs.
Fig. b. Swing the pole with the wrist.
Fig. c. Tap the pole on the snow and flatten the present stance ski (lower ski). Notice the change in body position, accomplished by lifting the stance foot to make it the free foot.
Fig. d. Touch the tip of the free ski to the snow and hold the ski tail off the snow.
Fig. e. Hold and pull the free ski and boot closer to the stance boot.
Fig. f. Balance on the new stance ski. Let the ski engage; do not steer or turn the stance leg or ski.

Cues for Success

- Touch the outside edge of the ski tip to the snow, and hold the tail a few inches above the snow.
- Touch the free boot to the inside ankle of the stance boot.

The Phantom Move

The mechanics of the Phantom Move were well known to me before the name evolved. I have used it in my skiing since I was 14, and I have coached Olympic athletes and National Ski Team members using this technique. The name came about by chance. I was coaching a group of instructors at Aspen. I told them I was going to make a turn, and I asked them to tell me how I made my skis turn. They were unable to come up with the answer, so I explained it to them, saying, "I gradually tipped my inside ski for the next turn to its outside, or little-toe, edge." I didn't lift the ski because I didn't want to give away the answer. I lightened and removed most of my weight from the ski and slowly tilted the ski toward its outside edge and the other ski started to turn as a result of the tilting action. When you do the Phantom Move in this way, it looks as though both skis turn together. One of the instructors piped up and said, "That's a phantom turn." I thought it described brilliantly the subtle, almost unnoticeable, mechanics. The untrained eye has difficulty seeing the actual movements when they are done smoothly with both skis on the snow. I later changed the name to the Phantom Move.

Release, Transfer, and Engagement

In a series of turns, the Phantom Move is a continuum of three movements of the free foot: tipping it toward its little-toe edge, keeping it light, and keeping its heel pulled in toward the stance foot. It creates the three components of linked turns: the release, transfer, and engagement. Tipping the stance ski toward its outside edge, flattening it to the snow, starts a new turn; these moves comprise the **release**. Lightening that foot until the ski lifts slightly off the snow causes balance to **transfer** to the new ski. Continued tipping toward the outside edge, combined with the balance transfer, pulls the stance ski on edge – the **engagement**. Pulling the free heel inward makes it easier to balance on the stance ski and increases the effectiveness of the tipping movement. I call the sequence of tipping, lightening and keeping the heel pulled in a "continuum," because those movements or efforts must be performed throughout the arc of a turn until the turn is complete and it's time to release again. They are not just one-time occurrences to start a turn.

Basics for All Skiers

Many of the undergraduate exercises may seem too simple at first. The black slope skier especially may decide to overlook them. However, I encourage all skiers to perfect them, for they will pay dividends later. These techniques are more challenging and eye opening than they may seem at first. It is my experience that few skiers are proficient at these exercises. Of those who are, many are already experts in most skiing situations.

Pulling Movements

Movements to pull the feet back and in are rarely introduced in ski lessons. There is little use or understanding of them in traditional skiing. Skiers may at first find these movements of PMTS Direct Parallel challenging. They are not difficult, just new. Pulling the free foot toward the stance foot at the release or beginning of a turn becomes second nature after practice. Pulling the free foot back under the hips is another pulling movement that will gain importance as you venture from groomed terrain. Start using and learning it as soon as you get onto snow.

Don't Turn the Skis

Let's get back to the issue of turning the skis. Remember, we take the phrase "don't turn your skis" seriously. In the description of the Phantom Move, I never said to turn your skis, feet or legs. Turning the skis requires steering or turning efforts with the large muscles of the legs, which diminishes balance by moving the skis out from under you and shifts the body's normally strong skeletal alignment to a weaker position. In fact, trying to turn your skis prevents you from progressing in your skiing. Look at *Figure 5-1* of the Phantom Move description and at the sequence below, *Figure 5-2*. Notice how the stance ski tail stays in line with the direction of the tip. The tail is never displaced or pushed out. This turn is carved or mildly brushed. These turns result from the use of PMTS. You will see them demonstrated in various ways throughout the book. The techniques that produce quick, efficient turns with balance use precise timing of releasing movements.

Fig. 5-2. Don't turn the stance ski

Biomechanical Advantage

- Balancing on the stance foot and tipping the free ski engages the ski's sidecut to make the turn.

Downhill Ski Edging

Throughout this book there is little reference to edging the downhill ski or pressuring the downhill ski. The movements of PMTS create balance on and grip by the downhill ski. I intentionally avoid too much discussion about downhill ski edging or pressuring because correct movements result in proper balance and edging. Emphasizing downhill ski edging and pressuring in the first third of a turn, the old-school approach embodied in the command "get an early edge," often produces exactly the opposite result: an early skid. As a PMTS turn progresses to the point where the skis are headed back in the new direction, pressuring the downhill ski can increase. Extending the downhill leg and tipping the free foot achieve pressuring and edging. Edging the downhill ski can increase after your skis have crossed the fall line and have started back across the slope. When your outside leg is extended, slight ankle movements to adjust edging can be effective. Press the ankle gently toward the medial wall of the ski boot to tip the ski further onto its big-toe edge. Avoid driving the knee to the inside whenever possible.

Performance Check

The performance test for this chapter is the Phantom Move with complete balance control. Complete balance control means that you can

- transfer balance before a turn begins
- balance momentarily on the little-toe edge of the new stance ski before it starts to turn
- hold the free foot off the snow throughout the arc of the turn until it is time to transfer for the upcoming turn
- turn as a result of the free foot's tipping toward its outside edge.

Break the Phantom Move into these small steps and manage your turns with the tipping actions of the inside ski rather than steering or turning the stance ski, and you will become successful as an all-mountain skier.

Chapter 6:
Free Foot Management

Refining the Release

The subtle actions of the free foot that truly make for expert skiing are rarely taught or discussed. Although the release that we covered in Chapter 4 is the basic PMTS method of finishing a turn and connecting to a new one, there is more to the transition then meets the eye.

I have seen students and instructors alike have problems with this part of the turn, even though many have read my first book. I also have been pleasantly surprised at how quickly the transition improves when the actions of the free foot are refined. Having read, and hopefully rehearsed, the movements described in Chapter 4, you know that the original downhill or outside ski becomes the free ski for the next turn. A successful release depends on that ski flattening. What you may not have practiced yet are the additional actions of the new free foot, beyond tipping to the outside edge and lightening. The free foot plays an important role in creating and modulating balance for the coming turn. By keeping the free foot close to the stance foot in transition, both side-to-side and fore/aft, balance on the stance foot is improved.

I teach our system almost daily to skiers and instructors, and I am continually amazed at how few skiers have that skill. They are even more amazed at how quickly they improve once they acquire the proper technique. The following photos show the concerted effort that must be applied to the movement of drawing the free foot toward the stance boot for the next turn.

Pulling the Free Foot into Alignment

a b

Fig. 6-1. Pulling the free foot into correct alignment with the stance foot

Hold the Free Foot Back

The skis and boots should remain parallel throughout the release, and they should stay even fore/aft. The ski tips and boot toes should remain side by side from the beginning to the end of the release. The tendency I see is for skiers to let the old downhill ski – the new free foot – slide ahead. Instead, maintain tension to keep the free foot pulled back under the hips. Flex that ankle and pull the free heel back under the hips. This prevents the inside foot from sliding forward. It is important to keep the free foot held back for the upper part of the turn. Developing this tension will make the turn transition easier. It should become part of your expert skiing repertoire.

De-emphasize Stance Ski Edging

Another important refinement during release and transition that is rarely developed by skiers is in the role of the new stance ski. Again, I must refer to the difference between traditional and PMTS instruction. Right from the beginning of instruction, this area is another in which the biomechanics of PMTS and traditional systems are opposite.

c

> **Cues for Success**
>
> • Touch the inside ankle rivets of the boots together, then tip the free foot.

Fig. a. Stand across the hill on the uphill ski.
Fig. b. Lift the downhill ski and pull it toward the stance ski and boot.
Fig. c. After making contact, tilt the free ski toward the outside edge. Although the downhill ski tail crosses over the uphill ski, this is not an intentional move. There is no effort to cross the tails. Rather, it results from tipping the free foot and holding it against the stance foot.

Traditional instruction is focused on early engagement of the inside or big-toe edge of the new downhill ski which is emphasized through the wedge progression. Wedge and wedge Christie turns require you to slide the tail of the new downhill ski away from the tail of the other ski before beginning a turn.

PMTS de-emphasizes the effort to roll the new stance ski to its inside edge. On gentle terrain, practicing the release with PMTS movements and the Phantom Move, delay engaging the new stance ski. Actually make an effort to keep the stance ski flat on the snow, rather than tipped onto its big-toe edge. The stance ski will change direction more easily as a result of free foot tipping, tilting, or rolling if it is kept flat to the snow. It will require no active steering, twisting, or displacing of the tail to make the stance ski turn. The actions and refinements of the free foot create "resultant turning" of the stance ski.

De-emphasize edging the stance ski at the beginning of turns and use correct free foot actions, and you'll be able to turn your skis completely within a ski's length of vertical distance. Speed control is achieved largely by reducing vertical distance in linked turns. Use the free foot actions and refinements of this chapter along with a less-edged stance ski to create tight short turns. Many skiers will need to "rewire" their movements and reactions in order to incorporate the delay in edging the stance ski. Focus on it, for once you have learned it, you'll have functional speed control for off-piste conditions.

What to Do When the Tips Aim Downhill

After the release, when the skis start to slide downhill, many skiers panic. To become comfortable and secure with the feeling of releasing, practice on a wide-open, gentle slope with few skiers. Make sure you are able to stop on this terrain, and that you are not afraid to let your skis run straight downhill on this slope. After you have released and let the skis drop to the fall line, use the Phantom Move of the inside ski to complete the full turn. To start the Phantom Move, lift the back of the inside ski. Focus on the back of the ski, while keeping the ski tip on the snow. The inside ski boot should be held close to the outside boot. Many skiers separate their skis at this point. Balance and stand on the outside ski.

Fig. 6-2. From a release, when your skis aim downhill, perform a Phantom Move

Explanation of Tipping Mechanics

Tipping can be defined as tilting or rolling the ski in a side-to-side direction. People often like to describe the activities that occur inside the ski boots to explain what happens outside. Here are the internal actions that create tipping of the ski: rolling a ski from its big-toe edge to its little-toe edge can be achieved by changing pressure from the inside edge to the outside edge of the foot. Articulating the ankle inside the boot, applying a lateral force on the sidewall, creates this action. The lateral force tips the boot and ski to or from an edge. Since this movement begins at the base of the kinetic chain, muscles higher up are recruited as needed to assist in the tipping actions. While this explanation may help you understand the mechanics of ski tipping, it is not the best way to teach this movement.

A continuing search for effective ways to describe and teach PMTS movements has led me to use external cues. I am convinced that this approach makes success more easily attainable for my students. However, I don't want to limit explanations to only external cues, when biomechanical or other information can provide additional motivation or understanding. I think it is important for skiers to have as complete an understanding of the mechanics as possible, for understanding can help some learn faster. I realize, though, that others are not motivated by that kind of information, preferring to access as little extra information as possible, while learning by experimenting with the movements. I have tried to accommodate both learning preferences in this book.

Additional Free Foot Exercises

The "Pole Press" and "Release with Ball Hold" exercises are designed to help you successfully release with the skis at the same edge angle. Both exercises will help you learn just how much effort or muscular tension is required to keep the skis parallel at release. This knowledge will be especially helpful when you venture off the groomed slopes.

Starting position for the Release with Ball Hold

Pole Press

The actions of the releasing ski are important for the success of the turn. After the release has begun, when the downhill ski from the previous turn is flattening and releasing and becoming the new free ski, you must continue to focus on that ski until you are well into the turn; this is the continuum of movement mentioned earlier. Retaining control over the releasing ski and boot in order to keep it in line with the stance ski after the release seems to be difficult to learn. The movements required to draw the free foot in toward the stance foot and keep it there do not seem to develop naturally, and they are rarely taught. Traditional teaching systems haven't incorporated pulling movements or actions of the inside foot. Though it may be new to your skiing, active pulling is extremely effective. This exercise enables the skier to develop the tension required to move the new free foot toward the stance foot and line it up for the turn.

For this exercise, you need a partner who will attach a ski pole to your downhill ski by placing the tip of the pole under the boot, between the boot and ski. Have your partner push the boot down the slope away from the other boot with the pole to create resistance. You must try to bring the boots back together by overcoming this resistance. Once you can duplicate that pressure to bring your free foot toward the stance boot in an actual ski turn, you will be ready to slice the snow.

This movement of drawing the old stance ski toward the new stance ski is critical if skiers are to become expert in bumps, crud and carving. It also has the same positive effect on skiers who ski on ice. Have you been unsuccessful on ice? You probably didn't have the free foot aligning forcefully enough with the stance ski.

Practice this pole press exercise until you are comfortable and think you can do the same thing with your boot after you release the ski from an actual turn.

a

Fig. 6-3. Press against your partner's pole to bring in the free foot

Cues for Success

- With the free boot touching the stance boot, have your partner push harder while you press inward to maintain contact between the boots.

Fig. a. Have a partner place his pole tip under your boot between the boot and ski.
Fig. b. Lift this boot and press it toward the stance boot.
Fig. c. Have your partner push the boot away.
Fig. d. Try to overcome your partner's push and press your lifted boot toward your other boot until you can make the boots touch.

Release With Ball Hold

Earlier, I said I would provide exercises to validate your progress and make sure you are performing the new movements correctly. The next series of photos demonstrates a foolproof way to test your abilities. You must practice making a turn while holding an object between your boots. Don't be discouraged if you aren't able to perform it perfectly at first. Holding a ball, glove or large car-washing sponge between your feet while you turn is not easy, but it ensures that your feet and skis are correctly positioned throughout the turn, with sufficient tension to keep them there in ungroomed snow. The sponge is the easiest of the three props to use; the ball is the most difficult.

Drop the Ball and You're Out of the Game

What are the factors that enable you to hold the ball in a turn?

- You must press the free boot against the stance boot.
- You must keep the boot toes lined up fore/aft.
- You must release the downhill ski first.

Fig. 6-4. Release holding ball between feet

> **Cues for Success**
>
> • Keep constant pressure with the free boot against the ball.
>
> • Keep the new stance ski flat on the snow until the fall line.

- You must prevent the uphill ski from rolling on edge prior to the downhill ski, or your boots will separate and you will drop the ball.
- You must make a precise balance transfer from one ski to the other and maintain balance throughout the turn.
- The boot and ski angles of both feet must be the same at all times.

If you can do all of these things in a turn then you are an expert skier and you pass this test! I have demonstrated this exercise to skiing champions as well as expert skier candidates. They found it very instructive. The exercise reveals any weaknesses in your technique and provides instant feedback about your skiing mechanics. A well-trained instructor can point out these weaknesses and help you change them.

I am demonstrating the exercise with a Nerf football. This exercise is difficult with a football because it has very little contact area. I found the large car-washing sponge most user-friendly.

Fig. a. Begin by standing across the slope. Place the ball between your boots and press the uphill boot against the lower boot just enough to keep the ball in place.
Fig. b. Begin to flatten and lighten the lower ski, shifting your balance to the upper ski. Press the lower boot against the upper boot to keep the ball in place.
Fig. c. Lift the free foot slightly off the snow. Pull the free ski back to prevent that boot from scissoring forward. Keep the new outside ski flat on the snow, not on edge.
Fig. d. Be patient with the turn; let the skis turn themselves. Continue to keep the outside ski flat on the snow.
Fig. e. Notice that there is no lead change or scissoring; the boots and ski tips are lined up perfectly.
Fig. f. The hard part is over. Press the free foot toward the stance boot as you tip it to the outside edge.
Fig. g. Both skis are tipped to the same edge angle as you stop.

e *f* *g*

Linked Turns with Ball Hold

This exercise is really useful. If you can make two consecutive turns holding the ball you are truly skiing with expert movements. If you use a traditional movement when you are in the position of *Fig. b*, you immediately will disqualify yourself from the exercise. No referee is necessary; the ball will roll down the mountain. A traditional movement here is flattening and putting the upper ski on edge first. You will notice in *Fig. d* that you must tip the lower ski onto its outside edge or it will catch in the snow. This exercise forces you to make the correct movements. The skis always must remain at the same edge angle. You may lift the free foot slightly to clear the snow, but you will have more chance for error this way.

Fig. a. Plant pole to establish balance for the release.

Fig. b. Lighten and flatten downhill ski of previous turn. Maintain constant pressure with new free foot toward new stance boot. This role change of the feet is critical. During the previous turn, the uphill boot was the free foot side that was pressing against the lower stance boot to keep the ball in place. Now the lower foot presses its boot uphill toward the new stance boot. Notice how the free ski boot and leg are tipped further on edge than the uphill stance ski and boot.

Fig. c. Stand balanced on the outside ski. Press the free foot toward the stance boot to hold the ball.

Fig. d. Continue tipping the free ski to establish the ski edge angles for the turn.

Fig. e. Hold the free boot back, even with the stance boot, or the ball will drop.

Performance Check

Using the large car sponge, you should be able to perform at least a release with ball hold in each direction to ensure that you manage your free foot adequately for off-piste skiing.

Cues for Success

- Squeeze the ball with the free boot against the stance boot.
- Deliberately flatten your stance ski to release.

Fig. 6-5. Linked turns holding ball between feet

Chapter 7:
Use the Force

Use Your Momentum to Reduce Your Effort

Lateral movements of the feet and ankles control ski edge angles, the rate of ski tipping, as well as turning. When we observe expert skiers, it looks as though their legs are turning in the same direction that the ski edge angle is tipping throughout a turn. The legs move toward the slope when the ski tips to a higher edge angle. The legs move away from the slope when the skis flatten to the snow. From the middle to the end of a turn, the body moves closer to the slope, inside the arc of the turn.

To begin a new turn, however, the body must move down the hill, away from the slope, out of the turn which can occur efficiently only if we begin releasing movements with the downhill ski. Tension in the downhill leg and the edge angle of the downhill ski resist the turning forces and keep the body inside the turn. If you release by flattening the downhill ski and relaxing the downhill leg, the turning forces will pull you in the desired direction, down the hill. Correct timing of the release makes it possible to use your momentum from one turn to move your center across your skis into the next turn.

Trouble arises when incorrect skiing mechanics are used instead of the release. Traditionally, the incorrect mechanics take the form of pushing off from the stance ski or extending from the uphill ski to move the body down the hill. After these movemetns are used, from that point on in the turn, inefficient compensating movements must be made. Skiers who use incorrect movements don't take advantage of the turning forces; therefore, they must incorporate compensations in order to extract themselves physically from the turn and launch themselves into the new turn.

When the turn is initiated properly through the release described above and detailed in Chapter 4, the skis tip to the new set of edges and the body moves into the new turn very quickly, with minimal effort. The idea is to minimize physical effort (relax the stance leg) by taking advantage of momentum and gravity. In effect, you are giving in to the turning forces that are pulling you down the hill. This causes your center to move across your skis and down into the next turn. Use the force; save your muscles.

Cues for Success

- Deliberately flex and shorten your stance leg as you flatten that ski to release.

Fig. 7-1. Use your momentum to start the new turn

Fig. a. Tip the inside ski to increase edge angles and turning.
Fig. b. Flex the inside knee as you tip to build the angles that resist gravitational and turning forces.
Fig. c. Begin to relax the legs and flex to reduce angles developed earlier in the turn.
Fig. d. Flex and pull up the knees toward the body. Flatten the skis with the pull of gravity and your momentum. Use the pole for stability.
Fig. e. Let the skis float to the surface and prepare to tilt the stance ski to its outside edge.

Tipping, Not Steering

Most instructors are trained to tell you that to achieve the turn of *Figure 7-1* you must steer your legs toward the hill. They will instruct you to rotate your legs away from the hill to start the new turn. Those movements do not create the turn I am demonstrating here. You may see how someone can be misled and made to believe that leg steering creates expert turns. The quest for this turn will be lifelong and unfulfilled if you use active leg steering. If you use the forces provided by the mountain and the tipping actions you can produce with your ankles and feet, you will create turns like the one I demonstrate.

The actions we just discussed are associated with letting go of the last turn. You will achieve an important breakthrough in your skiing when you realize that you should be expending more energy to keep yourself in a turn than to redirect your skis for the next turn. When you are able to do this, you will appreciate why I say that skiing should be effortless. You will no longer be concerned with turning your skis, just with how quickly you can relax, balance, and tip to make the transition.

The expert skier releases by relaxing the muscles in the stance leg. It can be difficult to tell a skier how to relax a muscle. Let's look at other, more obvious signs that a skier is relaxing the muscles of the leg to begin a release so we can develop an external cue that helps you learn to relax the stance leg. When you look at the photographs in this series, you will notice pronounced flexion of the legs at or near the end of a turn to begin a release. The flexing is initiated by the relaxing of the leg muscles. Skiers who want the release to happen very quickly will actually try to lift their knees and bring them into their chest. This is an important addition to your skiing for powder or in bumps to absorb pressure and change direction.

Practice Relaxing with Leg Flexion on Groomed Terrain

The next exercise is to link short turns on groomed terrain with a distinct relaxation and flexion (shortening) of the legs as you release. Perform the flattening and lightening of the old stance ski as you flex both legs. Keeping the legs in contact along their length will help the skis to work in unison. As you develop confidence in the timing and the movements, try this exercise on steeped terrain, where you'll be more aware of the flexion pulling your body downhill over your skis.

The photos on the next page may appear to be spread out because the release seems to take a long time to perform. Looks are deceiving — the release actually happens very quickly. The photos are spread out so that you can see the individual frames. If the individual frames were located correctly according to the turn, they would almost be stacked in a pile.

Fig. 7-2. Short turns with flexion at release

Fig. a. Begin to relax the leg muscles.
Fig. b. Prepare for the pole plant.
Fig. c. As soon as you feel the legs flex and the skis flatten, pull your knees aggressively to your chest.
Fig. d. Here I timed my pull with a slight bump to get an "air transition." This same move can be done in the bumps for spectacular air turns.
Fig. e. To land correctly for the new turn, tip the new free foot to the outside edge and pull that foot back.
Fig. f. Tip the free foot and keep it pulled in and back against the stance foot.
Fig. g. Managing the actions of your free foot will set you up perfectly for every turn.

Cues for Success

- Pull your knees up toward your chest to achieve leg flexion.
- Pull your free foot in and back to maintain contact with the stance foot.

Biomechanical Advantage

- Relaxing the stance leg and flattening that ski uses reduced energy and effort to begin a turn.

Chapter 8:

Weighted Release

The "Weighted Release," developed in PMTS Direct Parallel, is a sequence of movements designed to improve your turn transition technique. Keeping weight on the stance ski as it tilts to its outside edge reduces your dependence on big-toe, or inside, edge engagement, and internal femur rotation. The Weighted Release moves the body into the turn with assistance of "the force". We teach it to skiers who are ready to advance to expert status.

Watching skiers every day on the slopes gives me new ideas. I see their attempts to create proficient, fluid movements hindered by interruptive ski braking and gross, body-swinging actions. In an effort to solve these problems and provide immediate solutions, I develop exercises and movements that can be done quickly and easily. The Weighted Release is such an exercise. If you learn to perform the movements of this exercise as prescribed, you will become less dependent on big-toe, inside edge engagement, and you will have ultimate control over how much time you spend in transition between turns. There is an added advantage for knock-kneed skiers: the Weighted Release can reduce the tendency to ski knock-kneed. The Weighted Release also eliminates the step-off or push-off from the downhill ski that many skiers use at the end of a turn to project their bodies uphill into the next turn.

The problem knock-kneed skiers have is that they can't grip, or achieve enough edging, until their outside leg has rotated so far inward that their knee points at their inside leg. This extra internal rotation that they require to get an edge puts them in an "A- frame" position. The same is true for skiers who use leg steering and rotation to direct their skis. Often these skiers look knock-kneed but aren't. They actually have twisted the ski out from under the hips until they no longer have edge grip.

Normally the only way out of the situation is by stepping or pushing the uphill ski up and out onto its big-toe edge. These energy-intensive movements are limiting in all-mountain conditions and are hard to overcome. The Weighted Release can help to change these old movements. It enables skiers to keep the skis at the same edge angle during the release and engagement for the next turn. Many skiers, once they achieve edge grip, have great difficulty letting go of it. Holding onto that edge, not releasing it, keeps the body up the hill. Fluid skiing in powder, bumps, or steeps requires learning how to let go of the mountain. The Weighted Release will help you discover how easy it is to enter the next turn when you let go of the mountain. When properly executed, the turn happens almost effortlessly; that's why this exercise is so powerful. The Weighted Release leaves the skier no alternative but to move the body into the new turn. As you develop your Weighted Release, you'll be accessing the force as described in Chapter 7.

The first movement initiating a new turn should always be made by the stance ski of the previous turn. The ski closer to the bottom of the mountain is the downhill, or stance, ski. The other ski is the uphill, free, or unweighted ski. The stance ski is on its big-toe edge near the end of a turn. Watch and use that ski!

Make the initiating movement for the new turn by flattening the stance ski. First, relax the muscles of the stance leg — that will flex the leg slightly and allow the ski to come away from or off of its edge. Help the ski flatten by tipping the foot flat. Stand on the downhill ski; don't lighten it or shift your balance from it, as you would do in a regular release. This stance is what makes this a *weighted* release. As you flatten the stance ski, the uphill ski flattens along with it. Control the flattening of the uphill ski to maintain it at the same edge angle as the downhill, weighted ski. You can keep the uphill ski light or slightly weighted but both skis should be tipping at the same rate.

Fig. a. Through the end of the turn, balance on the downhill ski. The pole tip is already swinging for the pole plant.
Fig. b. Prepare the pole to tap and begin to relax the stance leg.
Fig. c. Flex and flatten the lower ski first; let the upper ski follow.
Fig. d. Keep the same amount of pressure on the lower ski as you had through the turn.
Fig. e. Bring both skis flat at the same time.
Fig. f. Begin to lighten the inside ski to make it the free foot.

Biomechanical Advantage

- The Weighted Release keeps your body moving into the next turn.

Fig. 8-1. Actions of a Weighted Release

Cues for Success

- Stand on the downhill ski as you flatten it.
- Relax and flex the stance leg as you flatten it.

Weighted Release with Lifted Uphill Ski

As mentioned earlier, knock-kneed skiers have difficulty letting go or rolling the downhill ski to the little-toe edge. It is more than just a knock-kneed skier problem; it is almost a universal problem. Even well trained, experienced skiers can be seen in a knock-kneed position at the end of turns. The combination of proper boots, alignment and movement can reduce even the most severely knock-kneed skier's A-frame position.

This exaggerated version of the Weighted Release, with the uphill ski lifted, is another step toward learning to let go of a turn so you can transition quickly into the next turn. Both approaches to the Weighted Release result in extraordinary benefits. Skiers who have difficulty moving their bodies into the next turn should practice both versions of the Weighted Release to appreciate and develop the feeling of letting go and transitioning into the next turn.

The lifted Weighted Release is like the previous Weighted Release, but with more emphasis on keeping all the pressure on the stance ski as it transitions to becoming the inside ski. To practice this exercise, lift the outside ski as you enter the turn, making the beginning of the turn on your inside ski. There is no balance transfer to the other ski during transition. Remain balanced on the stance ski during the edge change. If you're having trouble starting the turn, pull your lifted ski back so that the boots are even fore/aft. This will pressure the ski tip sufficiently to help the turn begin.

d *e* *f* *g*

Cues for Success

- Balance only on the downhill ski throughout the release.
- Keep the lifted boot even fore/aft with the stance boot.

Fig. 8-2. *Weighted Release with lifted uphill ski*

Fig. a. Finish the previous turn by relaxing and flexing the stance leg.
Fig. b. Continue to stand on the downhill ski as it is flattened.
Fig. c. Tip the downhill ski to the outside edge while standing and balancing on it.
Fig. d. Use the inside pole to help maintain balance by dragging it on the snow.
Fig. e. The outside ski is still completely light.
Fig. f. Turn and balance on the little-toe edge of the inside ski.
Fig. g. Lighten and lift the outside ski. Keep it lifted until the end of the arc. At the end of the arc place the outside ski on the snow and transfer pressure and balance to that ski. Begin the next lifted Weighted Release by balancing and staying on that ski.

Biomechanical Advantage

- Balancing on the downhill ski throughout the release automatically brings your body downhill over your skis to start a turn.

Performance Check

The Weighted Release can occur only if there is no balance transfer during the transition. Weight and balance remain on the old outside ski while you tip it to the outside edge. The outside leg must relax and flex to begin the roll of that ski to the new edge. The transition happens on the edges of the downhill ski. The edge change is from the inside edge to the outside edge of the same ski. The other ski, not weighted, follows. Once the stance ski of the previous turn comes to its outside edge it becomes the inside ski of the new turn. Standing on the previous downhill ski as you roll it to its outside edge may sound opposite to everything you have been told — and it is — but the exercise is invaluable, as it forces the body to commit downhill into the next turn. This transition that makes your body cross downhill over your skis is essential for all-mountain skiing. When you are able to begin turns with the lifted upper ski Weighted Release, you will have achieved the next required step in the Undergraduate Course.

Midterm Performance Check

You are sure to have tested your short turns before you come to this "midterm performance check," which is an important step in learning. There are many ways to test or gauge your success with your turns throughout the Undergraduate Course. Before you continue with the Undergraduate Course and learn the refinements needed for true all-mountain conditions, you should be able to ace the following short-turn test.

Short-Turn Test

On the steepest blue terrain you should be able to make 15 short turns in a space no wider than a cat track without picking up speed. The path left by a groomer is an ideal width corridor. Connect the turns without a traverse before the release. The vertical distance you cover in a single turn should be no more than two ski lengths. Keep the same speed for the whole run. If you can perform this exercise, you have a functional short turn, ready for the enhancements that will take you off-piste. Typically, skiers who have learned PMTS require two to three full days of concentrated effort to perform short turns with a controlled release. This may seem like a long time, but it's worth the effort. This short turn is the basis for all-mountain skiing.

Chapter 9:

The Float

Pause Between Release and Engagement

Learn to float and your life will change. I'm tempted to begin every new component or movement series in PMTS with the claim "It will change your life or give you a skiing breakthrough" because these techniques do exactly that. I watch the transformation of skiers daily. The float is an addition to your ski technique and understanding that will fit right in with the Weighted Release. The float is not so much a technique as a place between ski turns where time stands still. Have you ever wondered, "How can expert skiers look so controlled, no matter how steep or how uneven the surface? They never seem rushed." Now the secret is yours: they have a place of tranquility between turns, a point in time to look around and evaluate without rushing the next move. The float is accomplished simply by pausing tipping movements so you feel as though you are suspended in mid-air.

Even if you aren't a tennis player, you may appreciate the similarities between these aspects of the sports. Recreational tennis players are always rushing around trying to get to the ball and making it at the last minute with an off-balance swing. If you watch the best players, they never seem rushed when they hit the ball. They are always in balance as they swing the racket. The reason they are able to stay in balance comes from what I call the "moment of stop." Just as they swing the racket, their feet stop and the body stabilizes. As a result, the racket can take its prescribed path to make perfect contact with the ball. Players need this moment to adjust their eyes and establish balance in preparation for the fast-moving on-coming ball. Intermediate players don't have this moment in their game. Expert players can repeat it time and time again — that's one reason they rarely miss.

Let's find out more about this moment of stop for skiers. From the time your skis enter the bottom of an arc until the end of the turn, your body is up the slope or above your skis. The beginning of the next turn will change that. Your body will move across the skis toward the downhill side. During this process, the skis go through an edge change, or transition, initiated by the releasing action of the lower foot and leg. The skis are flat on the snow at some point in the transition, which is where the float occurs.

Fig. 9-1. Actions of the Float

a

b

c

d

e

The idea is to exaggerate and maintain the floating time. Release to bring the skis away from their edges, then pause the tipping of your inside foot and hold your legs and body at an angle of ninety degrees to the skis as they approach the flat. Stay over the skis and move with them as they continue forward, keeping them flat to the snow surface as long as you can. Delay the engagement for the briefest moment. At the moment of float, when your skis are flat to the surface, you are actually beyond vertical. Your body has moved downhill slightly over your skis so that you are perpendicular to the slope. There is no reason to panic. You aren't going to fall over. The pause in your releasing movements will make you feel suspended in mid-air, and you will experience the "moment of stop." Your body eventually will continue to move on its path to the inside of the next turn. As your skis roll onto their new set of edges, you will feel secure. Your skis will arc around the turn until once again your body will be above them.

Fig. a. Tip the inside ski and flex the inside leg to increase edge angle to the snow.
Fig. b. Balance on the outside ski and continue to pull the free foot back. The tipping and flexing actions have paid off to complete an aggressive short turn.
Fig. c. Begin to relax the leg muscles and flatten the ski.
Fig. d. The momentum from the previous turn will propel you over your skis.
Fig. e. Pull the knees up, start to flatten the downhill ski, and then pause the tipping action to let the skis float.
Fig. f. Keep both skis flat as long as you can — this is the float. Prepare to pull the new free foot in and hold it back under your hips.
Fig. g. To leave the float and continue moving your body into the turn, resume tipping by aggressively tilting the inside ski to its outside edge.

Cues for Success

- Relax, then actively flex the legs to release.
- Pause in tipping the free foot while the skis are flat on the snow surface.

f *g*

If you have a tendency to push or roll the upper ski onto its big-toe edge before the lower ski is on its little-toe edge, you won't feel the float. Experts can perform the float and therefore can ski powder, bumps and steeps without difficulty. The float gives you time to adjust your balance before entering the next turn. If you are out of balance at the end of the turn, as many skiers are, you have little chance to recover unless you use the float to regroup. Without the float, you are caught going from one out-of-balance turn to the next.

Do you see how this whole program fits together? We first focused on keeping both skis at the same angle to the snow during the release, which we accomplished by flattening the lower ski first. Then, the Weighted Release helps to connect more directly the flattening action of the downhill ski to the movement of your body across your skis in the transition. If you can do that, you are on your way to learning the float. It's just a matter of pausing briefly between release and engagement while your skis are flat on the snow. Practicing the Weighted Release gives you more control over the rate of your release and your ability to float between turns. With the float, you can adjust your balance and be prepared for any situation the mountain can throw at you. You're on your way to skiing bumps and powder successfully.

Fig. 9-2. See the float from the side view

Cues for Success

- Look for both skis to be flat at the same time in transition.

Fig. a. Finishing the previous turn, begin to relax the leg muscles.
Fig. b. Flex fully to absorb the bottom of the turn.
Fig. c. Relax the legs so the skis unbow.
Fig. d. Flatten the downhill ski to bring both skis flat to the snow, timing the pause to adjust the length of flat time.
Fig. e. Float with the skis flat. Prepare to become more active with inside boot pulling toward and holding to the stance boot.
Fig. f. Continue moving into the turn by resuming tipping of the inside ski to its outside edge.
Fig. g. Pull the free foot back to move the body forward over the skis.
Fig. h. Now you are balanced to begin flexing and tilting the inside leg and ski aggressively.

Performance Check

You can tell whether you are performing the float properly by looking at your ski tracks. The float occurs in the transition and is defined by the skis running flat on the snow between the release and engagement. When you examine your ski tracks between turns, there should be a section where you can see flat tracks from both ski bases, with neither ski tipped on edge. You should try to have the skis flat for at least a full ski length. If you have two flat tracks between turns with no edge impression, then you are performing the float correctly.

Chapter 10:

Upper and Lower Body Coordination

In ski books, there are countless mentions of the relationship between the upper and lower body under a variety of names. You may have heard it called a countered position, dynamic anticipation, upper- and lower-body separation, or blocked hips, to list just a few.

Upper- and Lower-Body Coordination, or "ULBC" as I call it, is the ability to coordinate counteracting movements of the upper body with turning actions of the skis, boots and legs. While good upper- and lower-body coordination makes it easy to ski with power, control, quickness and balance, many skiers have difficulty implementing this coordination in skiing. For that reason, I have put together a series of movement exercises that will increase your coordination. These are approaches I have tried that have proven to be effective for skiers. In conjunction with the movements of the feet and ankles, you will feel how ULBC exercises incorporate complementary movements of the upper body that will energize your skiing.

In PMTS we introduce upper- and lower-body coordination with an innovative approach. There is no single position that represents ULBC. Instead, it's a dynamic coordination of the upper and lower body throughout the turn. We teach ULBC while skiing, with movements and cues that produce this dynamic coordination rather than a static, ineffective position. You can use these movements immediately in all skiing situations. Simply put, the PMTS approach creates the movements that produce results and lets the body react to those counteracting movements.

Because the feet, ankles and shins are held securely by ski boots anchored to the skis, the movement of the lower body, from the thighs down, is influenced largely by equipment. You must learn to move your pelvis and upper body separately in response to lower-body movements. The feet are tipped to release and engage the skis. Increased tipping actions of the feet require that the thighs (femurs) rotate to keep up with the increasingly angulated skis. If the pelvis is held stable, both femurs can rotate under it without having the upper body follow. Remember in the descriptions of releasing how we referred to the rotation of the legs following the tipping skis, but described the upper body as remaining stable? Unfortunately, many skiers have difficulty creating this freedom of movement between the femurs and the pelvis.

Let's look back at some of the terms in skiing that have been used to describe ULBC. One is "countered position" and another is "upper- and lower-body separation." When the pelvis and upper body move with, or follow the rotation of, the femurs, few so-called counteracting movements are being used. Counteracting movements are being used correctly when the skier's upper body remains stable and quiet. It doesn't move, swing or rotate with the skis; thus the term upper and lower body separation. If the pelvis is held stable while ski edge angles increase through tipping the free foot, the thighs need not turn or steer in the direction of the turn. Counteracting movements that turn the pelvis away from the turn allow the body to increase mid- and upper-body lateral movements and therefore edge angles. When the body moves laterally into the turn and the pelvis is actively held or moved opposite to the turn direction, it minimizes or eliminates the need for femur rotation until the legs are flexed at the release. The introduction of shaped skis has changed technique in this profound way. Steering isn't a necessary part of skiing any longer, even at the intermediate level. Flexing at the bottom of the arc is an effective leg activity that complements modern ski technology. If you absorb the bottom of a turn by relaxing your muscles, the legs will flex. This is a progressive way to prepare for a release. As the pressure on the skis is reduced by flexing, the skis can be flattened easily. The ability to use the legs this way to release is dependent on how well you used counteracting movements at the beginning of the turn. If leg rotation or steering is used rather than counteracting movements early in the turn, the shaped ski design has less influence on the turn, and the ski is engaged less, reducing the possibility of the body moving inside the turn to help create edge angles.

We can start to feel and understand what stabilizing or counteracting movements mean by using indoor exercises. In my new book, *Ski Flex*, I introduce warm-up and stretching exercises that develop upper and lower body coordination while indoors. The indoor wall sit is one of these exercises.

Indoor Wall Sit

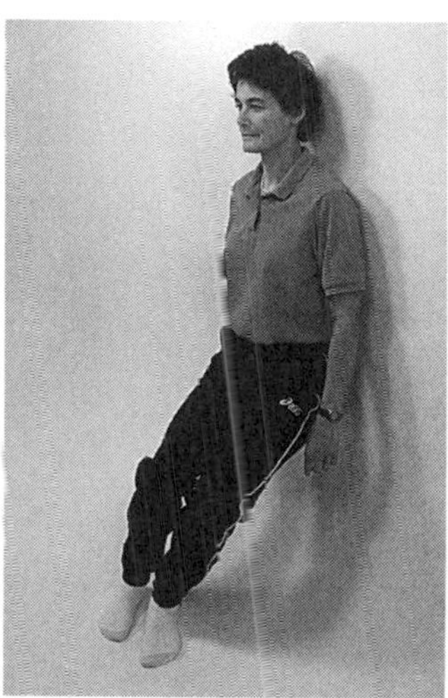

Fig. 10-1. Indoor wall sit

When sitting against the wall with flexed legs, you can begin to experience upper- and lower-body coordination. Turning your feet to one side, take note of how your legs move under a stable pelvis. Keep your pelvis and shoulders in contact with the wall. Place your arms against the wall to stabilize the upper body. Try to make counteracting movements with the hips by holding the pelvis against the wall before you turn your feet in a new direction. This movement sequence is the similar to what you will feel when the skis turn and your legs want to follow the turning skis. By counteracting the turning skis with the movement that keeps the pelvis flat on the wall, you will set up to develop body angles rather than knee angulation. Counteracting movements allow for a quicker, more powerful direction and edge change at the release. Because counteracting movements coil the body like a spring ready to let go of its energy, as soon as the release begins, the legs follow the flattening skis. Counteracting movements at the pelvis should be initiated immediately as, or just before, the skis begin turning.

The Poles and Upper and Lower Body Coordination

I have read most of the books on ski technique published over the past 20 years. Few, if any, accord pole use its true, deserved significance, which is an oversight, as skiers need expert pole use for expert skiing.

a

b

Fig. 10-2. Expert pole use for expert skiing

Fig. a. Prepare well ahead of the release with the pole swing.
Fig. b. Plant the pole and use it as a third point of contact for support and balance through the float.

Pole use has a major influence on upper and lower body coordination. However, integrating them can be tricky. Should pole use be developed before learning upper and lower body coordination? Is either more important and should one be learned first, or can they both be learned together? I hate to complicate the teaching, or leave open a point that might be misconstrued, but here is a dilemma: because coordinating the upper and lower body in skiing is largely supported by proper pole use, I feel that a correct pole plant should be developed first. I have seldom, if ever, encountered a skier who effectively coordinates the upper and lower body without a well-developed pole plant. On the other hand, I have never witnessed a skier with incorrect or mistimed arm and pole action achieve coordinated upper- and lower-body movement. So a correct pole plant can make upper and lower body coordination easier to learn.

Cues for Success

- Hold the hands still while swinging just the basket of the pole.

Every sport has its key instruction cliché. In tennis, it's "keep your eye on the ball"; in golf, it's "keep your head down as you hit through the ball." Skiing has it own set of teaching clichés. One that applies to pole use is "don't drop your inside hand." With this negative instruction, it is no wonder the suggestion is rarely heeded. Most people respond better to "keep your hand up", a modified version of this cliché.

This suggestion is valid and provides several sought-after benefits: better edge grip, carving control and upper-body stability. Before you work on keeping the hand up, you might want to know where your hands are during your turns and poling action. Find out immediately using a skiing partner.

Pole Use Test

Have a friend or family member ski behind you as you make short turns. Instruct your partner to give you immediate feedback on your hand position using a loud voice. Here is how it works: if both of your hands stay in the proper position, to the side of the body as you pole plant, your hands should stay visible to the skier behind you. The skier following shouts out "yes," to provide positive, immediate feedback. If the hand planting the pole disappears in front of your body, your partner immediately responds by yelling "no." As you make turns, the word "no" will indicate to you that your hand has moved from the side of the body to the front, obscuring it from the view of your skiing partner (who continues to ski behind you). You will have immediate feedback about your hand position and poling method. Over-rotation and reaching with the hand both cause the hand to disappear. The pole plant should be a swing of the pole tip, not the all-too-common forward driving action of the hand. See photos of this test in action on the following page.

Fig. 10-3. Test of pole use

Fig. a. Here's the correct pole hand and arm position – both hands are visible from the rear as the pole plants.
Fig. b. Elbows are bent, and hands are out to the sides.
Fig. c. Both arms are visible. Their position changes little from frame to frame.
Fig. d. Pole swing begins. The basket swings forward while the hand remains in place.
Fig. e. Inside hand and pole (here, the right) are up and forward.
Fig. f. Pole tip points downhill before plant.
Fig. g. Pole is planted – both hands are visible.

Fig. 10-4. Expert skiers have a relaxed arm position, and use counteracting movements of the hips early in the turn. Steering or turning the skis does not produce this result.

Effective Hand and Arm Position

One of the most misleading instructional cues I hear on the slopes is "keep your hands forward." Although this is well intended, it still causes many problems. Pushing or holding the hands forward is unnatural and actually makes the skier's shoulders and arms stiff. Expert skiers have a very relaxed arm position. Keep the elbows bent, hands to the side and shoulders relaxed.

Holding and Swinging the Poles

What is the secret to achieving a relaxed arm position? Try these tips. Bend the elbows so the forearm is angled slightly toward the upper arm, and keep the hands to the side of the body rather than forward. Now with just a slight lift of the elbows, you have a relaxed, consistent useful arm and hand position.

From this position, use your wrist to swing the tip of the pole forward and downhill for the pole plant. Review the photos and notice how the arms stay in the same place, but the pole tip moves a long distance. Using this method will quietly and properly position your pole, hands and arms.

With your hands and arms in this position, try the test again. After several series of turns, you should be able to adjust your pole swing. If you still are not able to make turns in which your observer becomes a "yes man," your hand is still disappearing to the front of your body. You may need a pole swing makeover. The test gives you an instant status report about your pole plant mechanics. Although we will review pole use here, additional information and other approaches can be found in two of my other books, *Anyone can be an Expert Skier* and the *PMTS Instructor Manual*.

Before attempting to develop upper and lower body coordination, try to establish a proper pole plant rhythm. As soon as one pole touches the snow, the other pole basket should start to swing forward, and so on. If this becomes too difficult, you can work on the upper and lower body coordination exercises without using any pole plant. If you prefer to learn upper and lower body coordination first, that's fine; take up the pole plant afterwards. The order of presentation in this chapter is pole use first, then upper and lower body coordination. If you feel you want to learn pole use first, read on; if you want upper and lower body coordination first, skip this section for now and come back to it after reading the next section.

Once you have integrated upper and lower body coordination with a pole tap, you are on your way. There are few experiences that can equal the thrill of controlled floating of your skis over powder. Without command of upper and lower body coordination and pole plant, achieving that level of expertise will be difficult, if not impossible. The upper body must be well balanced and solid to achieve the "float" in powder. A well-developed pole plant and upper and lower body coordination provide this solidity. Skiing powder without the solid pole plant and coordinated upper and lower body is like racing the Indy 500 with street tires. You can get around the track, but you are bound to skid into the wall at some time. The natural reaction is terror; driving a car in these conditions is not a pleasurable experience. I have skiers who tighten up from fear when they get in powder due to previous, unsuccessful experiences. Face plants and fear are reduced when a skier combines the float, a pole plant, and upper and lower body coordination.

Review

If the timing of your pole swing is off, or if the swing creates rotation of the upper body, then it must be changed. If you are pushing your pole-planting arm forward and at the same time trying to control hip rotation, for example, you will find it very difficult to perform these movements in tandem. An incorrect arm action rotates the shoulders, which helps rotate the hips; therefore, you are fighting your own movements. Now you can see why the pole use test is so effective: it gives you immediate feedback about your pole habits. To stabilize your upper body in powder and bump skiing, the pole plant needs to have purpose and must be done in a strong, deliberate fashion.

Fig. 10-5. Holding and swinging the poles properly make it easier to ski the ungroomed

Fig. a. Prepare early for a stabilizing pole plant – the pole is in position, pointed downhill, prior to planting.

Fig. b. Straighten the elbow after the pole tip has pointed downhill.

Fig. c. Plant the pole and release the skis (the legs have relaxed and flexed, and the skis are flattening to the snow). The body should move as a unit toward the pole as it sinks into the snow.

Fig. d. Use the pole to stabilize the body during the float, where the skis come to the surface. Hold the pole firmly so it can provide support.

a

Cues for Success

- Swing the basket forward early so it points downhill momentarily prior to planting.
- Hold your pole firmly so it can support and stabilize your body.

b

c

If it looks as though I'm vaulting my body off the planted pole shaft in Figures c *and* d, *you're right. I am using it here to support my body.*

d

Exercises for Pole Use

Home Base

Where you normally carry or hold your poles and arms is called "Home Base." Home Base should be a wide position, with hands at least 12 inches away and out to the sides of the body. If you keep a relaxed, bent elbow position with the hands away from the body, you'll be fine in most cases.

g *f* *e*

Fig. a. Hold the hands to the side, not stretched forward.
Fig. b. Use the wrist to swing the pole basket forward in preparation.
Fig. c. Plant the pole and immediately move the planted pole hand forward and over the pole tip so that it stays in "Home Base."
Fig. d. Start to swing the other pole basket forward.
Fig. e. The pole points downhill well ahead of the pole plant.
Fig. f. With hands in home base, hold the pole at the ready.
Fig. g. Tap the pole to begin the release. It signals flexing the legs and flattening the stance ski.

Biomechanical Advantage

- Home Base aligns the upper body for easier balance on the stance ski.
- Home Base diminishes rotation of the upper body and makes it easier to release into a new turn.

Fig. 10-6. Keep your hands in "Home Base"

Cues for Success

- Move the arms very little from Home Base.
- Prepare the pole early so you have time to point it downhill prior to planting.
- Always look downhill at the location where your next turn will finish.

Two Types of Pole Plant

The pole swing is thought of primarily as a timing device for starting turns, but it is much more. A pole plant can help solidify counteracting movements, it can stabilize the upper body, and it can reorient the body for the next turn. It definitely is an aid that complements the basic upper and lower body coordination exercises. Two basic types of pole plants can be used for different purposes. In the first type of swing, the flowing pole plant, the movement comes from the wrist and elbow. The shoulder is not part of the pole movement. Flowing plants are used on groomed terrain and in medium to large radius turns. The actual plant is more of a tap, and the tip of the pole is not held on the snow for very long. A stabilizing pole plant is used in steeps, short turns, bumps, powder or crud, where speed control and upper body balance and stability are necessary but are often jeopardized. In many cases, the stabilizing pole plant is held in the snow until the body has passed and turned around the point where the pole was planted.

The Flowing Pole Swing

The basic swing is good for everyday use on groomed or open terrain. The first thing to understand is that "pole swing" doesn't mean moving the pole grip or hand forward. On the contrary, to begin a swing, the hand and wrist are moved slightly up and toward the shoulder. Remember, we are trying to swing the tip of the pole, not the handle. The wrist and hand should move up only enough for the tip of the pole to be released in a forward swinging arc. When the tip of the pole is clear of the snow, you can swing the whole shaft using a small wrist movement. Swing the tip until it points down the slope, and hold it for a fraction of a second. When you have the tip pointing down the slope, aim it directly at the bottom of the mountain and extend the elbow until the pole tip touches the snow. Once the pole touches the snow, push the hand forward. Now your hand and the pole handle make an arc over the point in the snow where the pole tip is planted. Moving the hand forward in this way returns the hand to its original home base position. As the hand arcs over the planted pole, the other hand and wrist begin the swing movements to maintain uninterrupted rhythm.

Fig. a. From the home base position, bend the elbow and wrist to bring the hand toward the shoulder.
Fig. b. Swing the pole with the wrist to point it downhill.
Fig. c. Tap the pole tip in the snow.
Fig. d. Immediately move the hand forward over the pole tip to return to home base.

Cues for Success

- Bring the elbow in and the hand up.
- Use only the wrist to swing the basket forward.

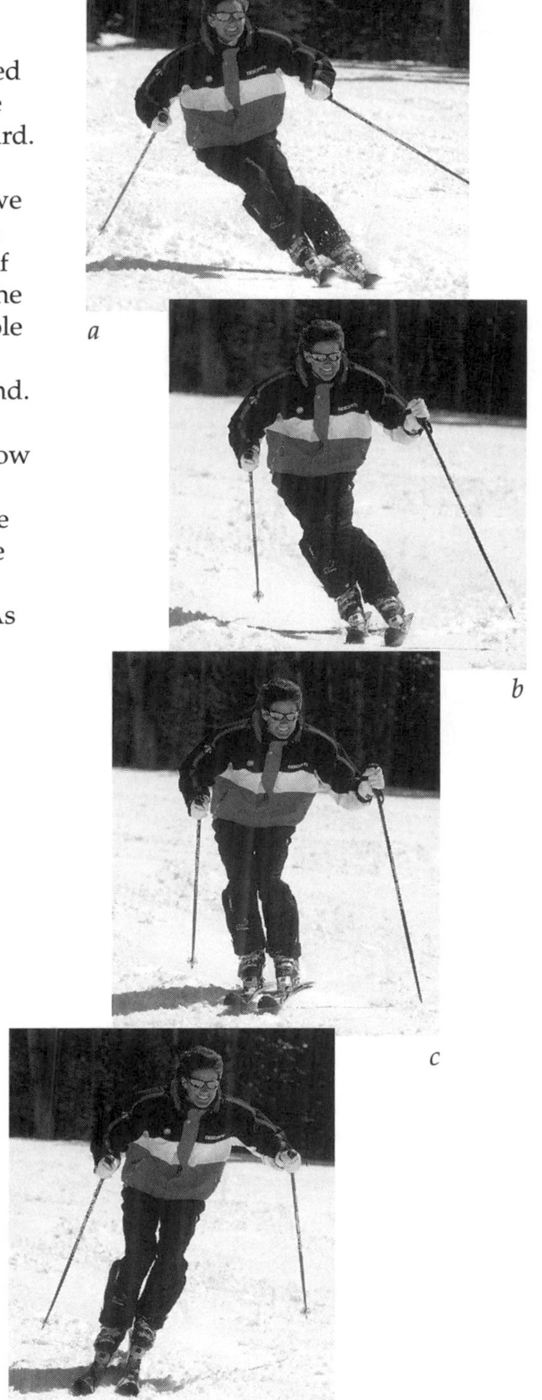

Fig. 10-7. The flowing pole swing

The Stabilizing Pole Plant

The second, more advanced type of pole swing is really the same but with a pronounced and more deliberate pole set in the snow. This swing is used on terrain where speed control is desirable, where you'll be completing your turns with the skis headed almost 90 degrees across the fall line. The stabilizing pole plant gives your upper body control and balancing assistance. The timing of this plant requires a longer pause in preparation for the turn, where you hold the pole tip pointed down the slope. The planting action is deliberate and delayed until your skis cross the fall line. Because the pole plant is held longer and more weight is applied, it helps move the upper body and shoulders down the slope, towards the planted pole and the center of the next turn, which helps line up your upper body for the next turn as you begin the tipping, releasing actions of the ski.

b a

Fig. 10-8. The stabilizing pole plant

Fig. a. Line up the upper body solidly to the fall line, plant pole firmly to stop upper body movement.
Fig. b. Release skis and use pole for balance during float. Keep the pole planted as skis continue by it.

There is another important demonstration here. In Chapter 5, I discussed the need to *not* turn the stance ski when starting a turn. Notice here how from *Figure a* to *b* my skis have flattened and released, but they have not changed direction.

Cues for Success

- Keep the hands in home base before and after the plant.
- Plant and grip the pole firmly so that it stabilizes the upper body.

Preparing for the Stabilizing Pole Plant

Fig. a. Develop the pole swing as the turn begins by bringing the hand toward the shoulder.
Fig. b. Use the wrist to bring the pole tip forward. Notice how there is little change in any other part of the body.
Fig. c. Flex the wrist to bring the pole tip higher, aiming it downhill. This action prepares for a stable transition.
Fig. d. Extend the elbow to help reach the pole into the snow. Hold it firmly.

Fig. 10-9. Preparing for the stabilizing pole plant

The slight delay and holding the pole in the snow longer maintains the upper-body position and keeps it from rotating in the direction of the turn, constituting an upper-body counteracting movement. In effect, counteracting movements of the upper body conserve energy and store it for use in the release. Keep the pole in the snow as long as you can while moving the other hand and pole forward into position for the next turn.

Cues for Success

- Keep arm and shoulder stable.
- Use wrist and elbow to swing the pole.

Pole Basket Push

The pole basket push is a great exercise for orienting the upper body level to the snow. It also reduces the amount of pole and arm movements of the upper body, which is called "cleaning up extraneous movements." Read the explanation carefully. The pole basket push is so contrary to many skiers' pole habits that they find the concept difficult to grasp.

The first part of the explanation is very simple. This exercise requires that you keep your pole tips forward of the boot toes at all times during the turns. You can feel yourself accomplishing this by pushing the pole tips along the snow. Do a straight run while holding your poles vertically and drag the tips along the snow. Use your wrists to create pressure on the pole handles to keep the baskets forward of your boots; don't let the baskets drag back along the snow, so that you can feel the resistance created by the pole drag that you'll have to counteract with your basket push. In the pole basket push exercise, continue to create the same forward wrist pressure with the inside pole, preventing the baskets from dragging backward. Your hands will be high and the pole tips will be to the side of the binding toe pieces.

Right after you make a regular pole plant, before you move past the spot in the snow where the pole is planted, lift the pole tip and push it forward (remember the wrist action from above) along the snow. Lifting the hand and flexing the wrist toward your shoulder is how this movement is accomplished. It requires that you keep pushing the bottom of the pole forward as you move through the end of the turn. Keep pushing the pole basket while you prepare the other hand for the next pole swing. It's as though both pole baskets are swinging forward, one to prepare for the plant, the other pushing forward along the snow to stay ahead of the boot toes. After you plant the pole on the other side, push its basket forward in the same way you did for the last pole plant. Using the pole basket push on both sides with both poles will keep the poles well forward of the boot toes and keep the hands and poles positioned higher by your hips. This technique results in very beneficial upper body discipline.

Fig. a. Set up the pole plant with a wrist swing.
Fig. b. Plant the pole and be ready to drag the tip forward on the snow before it gets behind your binding toe pieces.
Fig. c. Use the wrist to push the pole tip along the snow.
Fig. d. Press the basket forward and well uphill of the feet so it doesn't snag. Prepare the other pole for planting.
Fig. e. Swing the outside pole basket ahead for its pole plant, aiming the pole downhill prior to planting.
Fig. f. Plant the downhill pole and repeat the drag on that side.

Fig. 10-10. The pole basket push, shown with the right pole

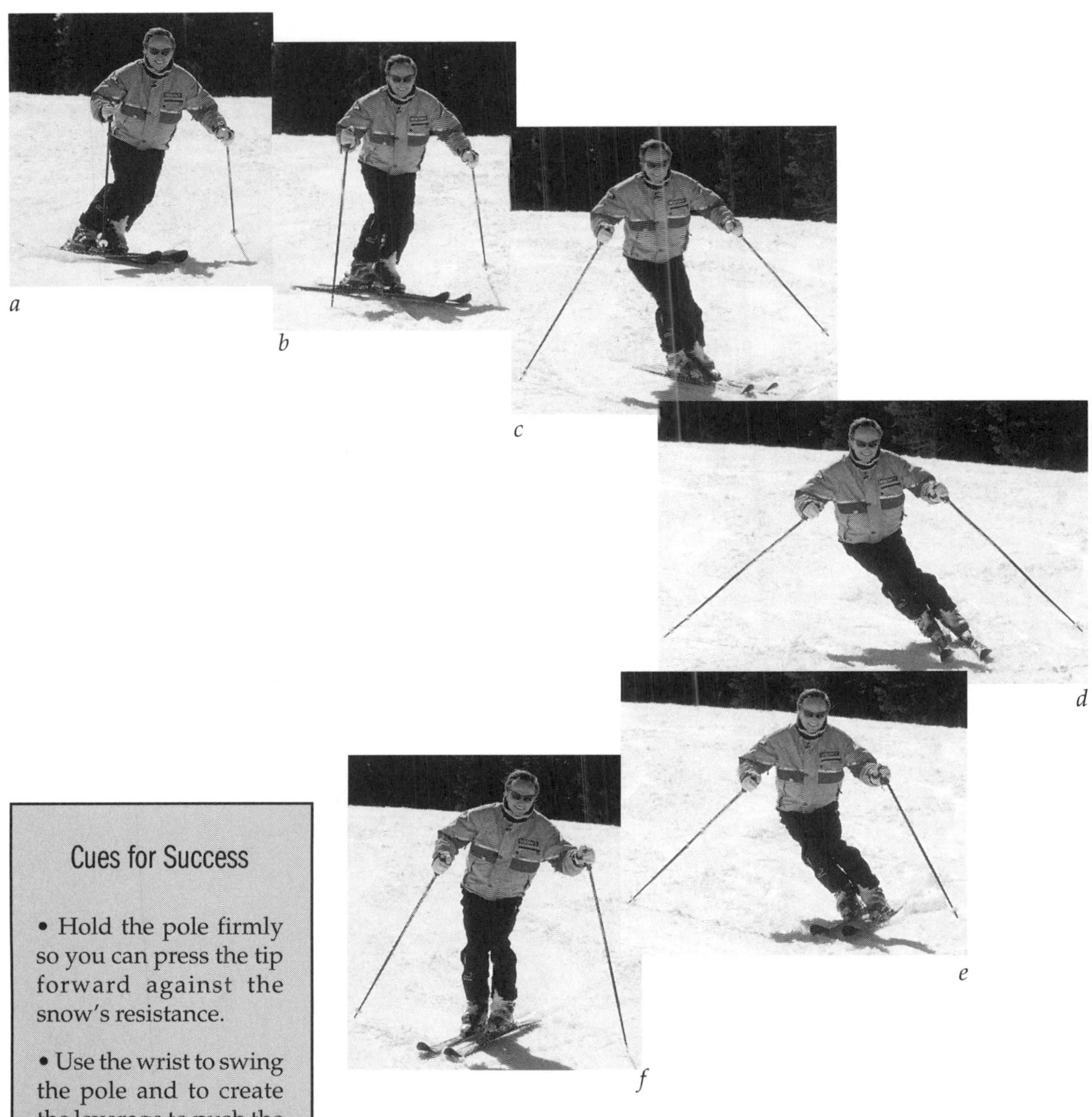

Cues for Success

- Hold the pole firmly so you can press the tip forward against the snow's resistance.
- Use the wrist to swing the pole and to create the leverage to push the tip forward along the snow.

Effective Pole Use Develops Upper and Lower Body Coordination

In short turns, to manage speed control and turn frequency, the pole movements must never stop. As one side is moving the pole into position for a pole plant, the other arm and hand prepare for the turn. After you plant the pole and you begin to move past the spot where the tip was planted, the hand and arm move forward, resuming their home base position. The inside arm is in the "strong-arm position" that maintains upper body position and stability. "Strong-arm" is a phrase I developed in the PMTS Instructor Manual. I point out what it is in the photos describing pole use. More terrain-specific pole use situations and descriptions will be illustrated as we move into the off-piste topics. I must reiterate that pole use has been largely ignored in skiing instruction. It is the one area in which you immediately can make big changes in your performance. Skiing more difficult terrain will not be fulfilling or enjoyable without well-developed pole skills.

Exercises for Upper and Lower Body Coordination

Building ULBC will take a two-pronged approach. The first set of exercises builds body balance and awareness. The second set of exercises builds the actual movements for dynamic turn-to-turn applications.

Counteracting movements, rarely used or understood by skiers, are part of the upper and lower body coordination program. Some form of a countering movement is part of every turn and is described by a turning action of the pelvis and upper body in the opposite direction of the turn. This movement counteracts and offsets the possible rotational movements created by the lower body as the ski's side cut engages to generate arcs. The counteracting movements can be active as in a steep energetic bump run where the upper body actually turns in the direction opposite to the skis, or the pelvis can be held stable to allow the femurs to follow the arc of the skis and turn under the pelvis.

The exercises introduced at the beginning of this section will also benefit your pure carving performance. Pure carving is a function of tipping the skis without slipping. The first set of exercises develops the body balance and awareness for riding on your edges rather than on the bases. Skidded turns have significant contact between base and snow. Carved turns have very little base-to-snow contact, unless the snow is soft. The carved turn on very hard snow is predominantly pure edge contact.

Let the Legs and Torso Become Independent

The beginning exercise is simple, safe and straightforward. It may remind you of the old Austrian starting position or traverse exercises that their ski schools used during the 1960s. Don't worry — this situation is temporary to loosen you up and make you aware of your mid-body range of motion. Make sure you look up the mountain to avoid traffic before beginning any exercise that takes you from the side of the slope into the slope.

Before you start moving, the upper body is turned in a pronounced manner, to face downhill. The skis are tipped onto their uphill edges. Hold yourself with your poles to prevent sliding before you begin to position the skis and upper body. Balance so you can stay upright; turn your uphill hip forward so that your backside is to the slope. When you are in balance, let the skis go. Let the skis run on their edges without turning or slipping. If you don't travel forward far enough across the slope, do the exercise again, but this time, begin by pointing your skis more steeply downhill. If you are on carving skis, you will notice they will immediately take you back up the slope, describing a round arc, leaving two thin edge lines in the snow. Because of their design, the skis want to scribe a semi-circle or half-moon on the slope and don't require any assistance from the pilot. This action is what we are trying to achieve when we say,

"let the skis do the work."

Edge Lock Traverse

Fig. 10-11. Starting position, edge lock traverse

Fig. 10-12. Skis scribing arcs in edge lock traverse

Start with the skis aimed slightly downhill, rolled on edge. Balance with the skis on edge and your back facing up the slope. Let the skis run. Tip the skis to a higher angle, turn your back to the slope, and lean out over the downhill ski.

Fig. 10-13. Edge lock traverse - emphasize free foot tipping

Fig. a. Traverse on your skis' edges with the skis pointed slightly downhill.
Fig. b. Balance while you ride the arc scribed by the ski edges.
Fig. c. Tip both skis evenly and sufficiently to prevent skidding.

Cues for Success

- Tip both skis evenly before sliding.
- Aim your back uphill.
- Look for clean sliced tracks in the snow to confirm your performance.

The secret is timing. PMTS instruction will tell you

"don't turn your skis, they should turn by themselves,"

without physical assistance. Lito Tejada-Flores, my good friend, refers to this effect of the skis turning themselves as the result and benefit of his emphasis on "dynamic anticipation". Although we may not call these actions or techniques by the same name, they are the same thing. We are referring to the same coordination of upper and lower body that we know is a component of expert skiing.

In the exercise, the idea is to keep the skis cutting the snow so they leave two clean, distinct edge cut lines on the snow. The only way you can achieve this amount of edge-hold is by balancing properly over the skis. If the upper body or pelvis rotates you will lose balance and the skis will skid. Most skiers require two or three tries in both directions before they feel the skis locking into the snow and carving an arc.

Garland Release with Reengagement

The garland release with reengagement is a refinement, test and more advanced version of the traverse edge lock. You have to be able to flatten and then reengage the skis while sliding forward.

Set up the same as for the previous exercise. Let the skis go. As you begin to slow down near the bottom or belly of the arc, when your skis are pointed across or slightly up the hill, release or flatten the skis to the snow. You will have to relinquish your edged or angulated body position to flatten or release the ski. "Angulated" means tipping the ski to a high edge angle. The "angulated body" results from balancing on that edge angle. Let the skis flatten completely until they redirect and start to point down the slope. When the skis become flat to the slope and your tips have aimed downhill as steeply as your starting position, reengage the edges and hold the skis on edge to finish a new arc. This

Fig. 10-14. Garland release with reengagement

Fig. a. Traverse with the edges locked on angle and cutting a clean line.
Fig. b. Flatten both skis, initiating with the downhill foot, and let the ski tips start to drop downhill.
Fig. c. Tip the downhill foot to the outside until both skis become flat to the snow.
Fig. d. Quickly tip the skis back on edge, initiating by tipping the uphill ski uphill and keeping the flat of your lower back facing uphill.
Fig. e. Hold the skis on edge and maintain balance.
Fig. f. Keeping your back aimed uphill and the skis on edge, let the skis run until you stop.

exercise is basically an edge release garland, with extreme body angulation. The reason for introducing extreme angulation is to make you familiar with a range of body motion that you may never have achieved before. Skiers rarely discover on their own how far they can or need to move to create aggressive body angles relative to the snow. Expert skiing on all terrain may require moving in these ranges. Expert skiers may reach the extremes of this range in split seconds when they ski quickly in bumps and while carving.

Cues for Success

- Tip the uphill ski and move your hip uphill to engage the skis without skidding.
- Keep the uphill ski pulled back so the ski tips are even fore/aft.

Straight Run ULBC Exercises

Now do the edge lock exercise from a straight run. With this exercise, you begin moving to the edges of the skis and riding on them. Try to put the skis on edge without skidding and then balance over the edges. As you increase the edge angle, move your body in the opposite direction from the turn. Just as you did in the traverse edge lock exercise, turn your backside slowly to aim to the inside of the turn. You will know when the skis engage as they may feel like they are on tracks or rails taking you for a ride. Don't panic: enjoy the sensation. Establish balance by increasing the amount of body turn in the opposite direction to the ski turn. Make sure you have less pressure on the inside ski — there should be just enough to leave a groove. Quick or aggressive movements will put you off balance, so take your time developing these movements. Once the skis have changed direction enough to feel the arc, gently and gradually bring them flat and start tipping to the other set of edges. Notice that you are skiing on all four of your edges from one turn to the other. Skiers who have alignment problems will have difficulty keeping both skis at the same angle. Don't give up; remember, tipping the inside ski is very difficult for a knock-kneed skier. Staying balanced on the outside ski is difficult for the bowlegged skier.

Make sure you choose a low traffic area on a flat slope for this practice.

a

b

c

d

e

f

Fig. 10-15. *Straight run ULBC exercises*

Fig. a. Start with the skis flat.
Fig. b. Tip the left ski toward the outside edge. Lighten it to have only slight contact with the snow.
Fig. c. Balance mostly on the right ski, and turn your back to the inside of the turn.
Fig. d. As soon as the skis engage and start along an arc, flatten them back to the snow.
Fig. e. Begin tipping the skis ever so slightly in the other direction while you prepare to turn the upper body in the opposite direction.
Fig. f. Tip the new inside foot into the turn and turn the upper body in the opposite direction.

Biomechanical Advantage

- Tipping with counteracting movements engages the skis without skidding.

Fig. a to b. From a straight run with skis flat, turn your upper body to the right and tip the left ski slowly on to its outside edge.

Fig. c. Stay balanced over the edges and let the skis track until they change direction.

Fig. d. Bring the skis back to flat with your body facing forward, as you started.

Fig. e. Tip your right ski onto its outside edge while you turn your body to face the left, with your back aimed to the inside of the new turn. Engage the skis cleanly.

Cues for Success

- Look at your tracks to gauge your performance. You should leave two clean arcs, then a brief section with two flat base tracks, then two new arcs, with no skidding or brushing marks.
- Turn the body before the skis tip on edge.
- Ride on the edges and let the side cut dictate the path.

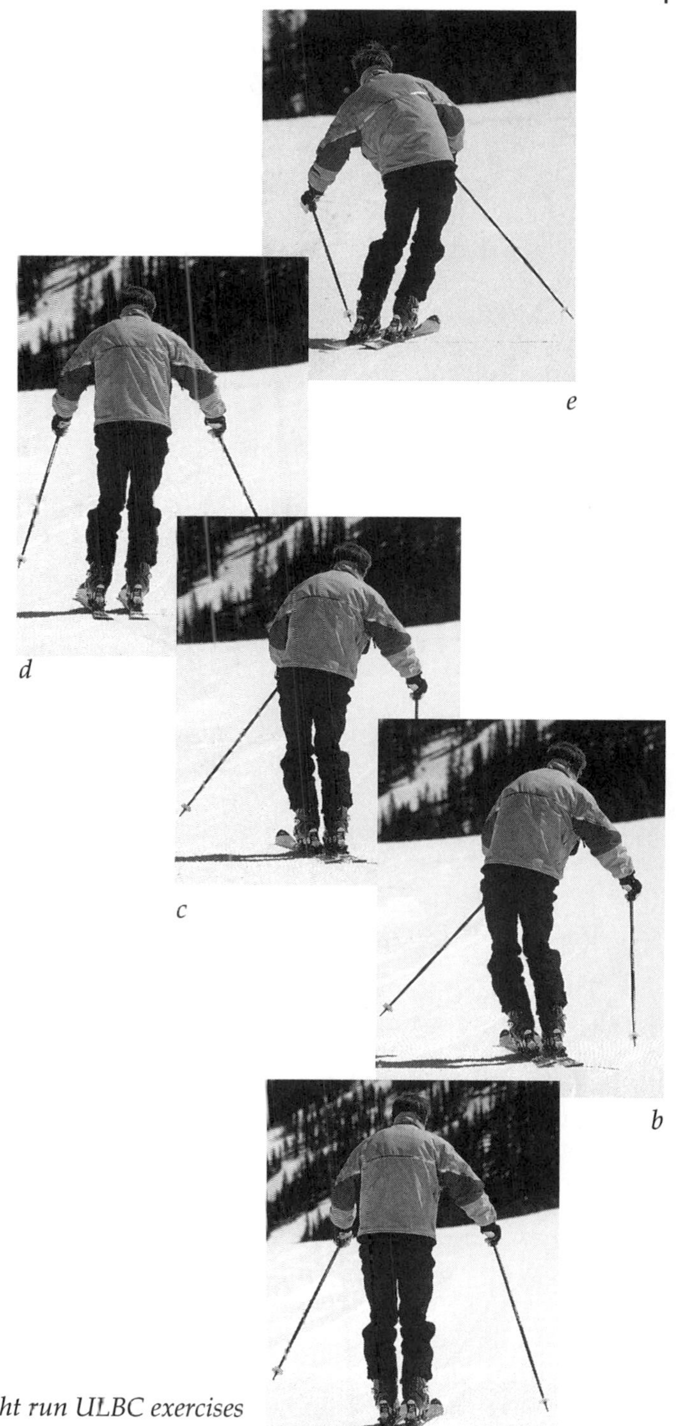

Fig. 10-16. Straight run ULBC exercises

I have taught the straight run ULBC exercise frequently to both advanced and high-level expert skiers. Even these skiers often require at least a run or two, sometimes an afternoon, to master the exercise. Start by gradually and progressively tipping the skis. To be very clear, I said tipping and I mean tipping only. Most skiers, whether they are aware of it or not, have rotation and skidding built into their every movement. Rotation is an unnecessary and debilitating habit that must be eradicated. Once you have completed the Undergraduate Course and can tip your skis and engage them without inadvertent skidding, I will demonstrate how you can increase the turning or redirecting of your skis using efficient and accurate movements. Skiing is traditionally taught with an overemphasis on rotary and steering movements, which results in body rotation and skidding skis, because skidding has been the only understood means to change ski direction, especially for beginning and intermediate skiers.

I recommend that you develop all the exercises in the series to a satisfactory skill level, as they will pay off when you encounter your first powder day. Learning the basics on a powder day is a frustrating waste of a potentially great day. Your friends are out shredding the snow and you are digging yourself out and cleaning your goggles. Try these exercises and learn to incorporate them into your skiing technique. The edge lock traverse deserves at least three tries in each direction before you start the straight run ULBC exercise. The straight run version deserves at least an afternoon. Check your tracks frequently to make sure you are practicing the right movements. If you have trouble leaving two clean arcs, practice the edge lock traverse.

Dynamically Coordinating Upper and Lower Body in Skiing

Now that you have practiced the exercises that help you isolate your upper and lower body and learn balance on cleanly engaged edges, you're ready to progress to the second prong of the ULBC. The next exercises help you coordinate your upper and lower body in linked turns in the manner that will take you off-piste with success. Use the range of upper and lower body movements you experienced in the previous exercises.

Arch/Hand Lift, Poles Horizontal

This exercise is one of the most effective from the upper and lower body coordination series I developed. I am unaware of any other instructors who use this approach. It can be included any time you are ready to begin coordinating your upper and lower body. The Arch/Hand Lift is a variation on the Phantom Move that adds a role for the upper body. Coordinating ski and foot action with upper-body counter tilting is the goal of this exercise.

If you have never practiced the Phantom Move in short turns, it might be a good idea to review and practice that first. Link short turns using the phantom lifting and tipping action with each turn. The first question I usually hear in response to this exercise is "Which foot do I lift?" First, think about lifting the arch rather then the foot, as this action will incorporate both the lightening and the tipping into one thought. Second, lift the arch of the foot in the direction in which you'd like to turn. If you want to turn right, lift the right arch. As an example of an external cue to help you gauge your performance, you might think, "show the base of your inside ski to the other boot." Balance and stand on the regular outside or stance ski. These should be short, shallow turns, with just enough direction change to head back across the slope. After a slight direction change, put the lifted arch or ski back on the snow and start lifting the other arch.

Once your short phantom turns are working well, you are ready to coordinate the lower body with the upper body. Hold your poles out in front of your shoulders as in the photos. Coordinate lifting the arch with lifting the same hand in the turn — i.e. right arch, right hand. As you begin lifting the free foot, lift the hand on the same side of the body. Keep enough tension in the arms so that lifting the hand also lifts the shoulder. You develop a functional relationship of the upper body to the lower body by coordinating these movements.

a

Fig. 10-17. Arch/hand lift, poles horizontal

b

c

d

Fig. a. Raise the inside arch and lift the inside hand at the same time.

Fig. b. Continue to tip the inside ski and keep the inside hand slightly higher.

Fig. c. Place the inside ski back on the snow, raise the other arch and lift the other hand.

Fig. d. Complete the turn by holding the inside hand high and keeping the inside arch lifted.

This combination of movements will swing all of your body weight over the outside ski; it will also create increased body articulation. You should start to feel a difference in the way your body reacts to turns. The first sensation many skiers report is a pinching at the lateral part of the ribs and hip on the side over the outside ski. This feeling makes complete sense as the exercise tips your upper body toward the downhill side, in turn, stretching the uphill side of the body. Notice in the carving section of the book (Chapter 12) how the upper body is still slightly angled toward the outside ski despite the extreme body angles attained. Keeping the body angles slightly toward the outside ski increases edge grip, especially on hard and icy snow. In the carving section of the book you will notice the emphasis on moving the hip and mid-body into the slope, but not the upper body, head or shoulders. This exercise will help you develop this ability. Leaning the upper body accomplishes very little except loss of balance. Your upper body will develop tremendous angles to the surface after you achieve lateral balance.

Fig. a. Lift the new inside ski.
Fig. b. Tip the inside ski to its outside edge and raise the inside hand.
Fig. c. Set the ski back onto the snow and bring the hands to level.
Fig. d. Begin to lift the right ski and right hand.
Fig. e. Increase the lift of the right hand and the right arch through the turn.
Fig. f. Increase the tipping of the lifted ski to increase the body angle to the slope.
Fig. g. A slightly lower outside hand and higher inside hand is a good indication of a stable body.

Biomechanical Advantage

- Coordinating your upper body with the lifting of the free foot establishes solid balance on the stance leg.

Cues for Success

- Hold the poles out in front of you.
- Lift the arch and hand together.

Fig. 10-18. Straight run ULBC exercise

Fig. 10-19. *Arch/hand lift, proper pole position*

a

b

c

d

Arch/Hand Lift, Proper Pole Position

Once you have coordinated the arch lift with the horizontal pole lift, you are ready to hold the poles in their normal position and try the exercise again. The idea here is to feel the extra edge hold and angulation that can be achieved by upper body coordination. Hold the poles away from the body, and as you lift the your arch/ski, lift the hand on the same side. The movements of this exercise feel extreme, but when I look at the photos we took after the photo shoot, I am always amazed at the excellent body position that the exercise provides. I don't think we should ski every day using this extreme upper body outward tilt, but the exercise conveys to skiers how much more tilt is available in their regular skiing.

Biomechanical Advantage

- The reaction of the body to the arch and arm lifting engages the ski's sidecut without skidding.

Fig. a. Keep the hands level in transition.
Fig. b. Lift the back of the inside ski and start tipping it.
Fig. c. Lift the inside arm.
Fig. d. Flex the legs to release.
Fig. e. Prepare to lift the back of the new inside ski. Here, in transition, the hands are level again.
Fig. f. Lift and tip the inside ski, and lift the inside arm.
Fig. g. The inside ski is tipped, and the inside arm is slightly higher. This position is truly balanced.

e *f* *g*

Cues for Success

- Lift inside hand, arm, and shoulder.
- Lift the arch and arm together.

Performance Check

The performance check for this chapter has several components. Coordinating the upper and lower body is critical to success in any "graduate conditions" — ungroomed snow or high-angle carving.

Pole Use

Enlist a friend to help you judge your pole use. You should be able to pass the pole use test in linked short turns on groomed expert terrain: when viewed from behind, your hands will be visible at all times on each side of your body.

In linked short turns on groomed intermediate terrain, you should be able to perform flowing pole plants. Have your friend watch to be sure that your pole touches the snow just before your release, and to be sure that the rhythm of pole swing and turns remains constant for at least 10 turns.

To be prepared for the Graduate Course, you must link at least 10 turns on groomed expert terrain with stabilizing pole plants. Have your friend watch to be sure that your pole is firmly planted before your skis release, and to be sure that your speed remains controlled and constant over the 10 turns. At the end of each turn, your skis should be pointed across the hill while your upper body faces downhill.

Upper- and Lower-Body Coordination

The performance check for ULBC comprises two tasks. First, you should be able to perform a garland release with reengagement to a locked-edge traverse in both directions. Second, you should be able to perform the straight run ULBC exercises with a locked-edge engagement in both directions. For both of these tasks, you can judge your own performance by examining the tracks your skis leave on the snow. When you perform the exercises correctly, you'll see that the skis roll onto edge without any skidding or sideways travel of their tails. In the straight run ULBC exercise, you should see two clean edge arcs, then a momentary flat track from the ski bases, then two more clean arcs.

Poles and ULBC

Check that you can coordinate your body and the pole swing by performing the arch/hand lift with the poles in their regular positions. You should be able to link at least 10 turns on groomed intermediate terrain without gaining speed.

Final Performance Check

Congratulations! Achieving upper- and lower-body coordination is the final step before you proceed to the Graduate Course — carving, bumps, powder, or all three topics. If you have succeeded at the performance checks for each chapter in the Undergraduate Course, you're ready for the final check. All that remains is the Linked Release Test.

Linked Release Test

For the final test, you should be able to perform at least 10 linked releases, coming to a complete stop after each release. Any of the releases from the Undergraduate Course (two-footed, weighted, or from uphill ski) is fine as long as the skis remain parallel throughout the exercise. The requirements are:

- a stabilizing pole plant is in place as you come to a stop
- you stop within two ski lengths
- the arc of your turns is less than two ski-lengths wide.

Graduation!

Upon successfull performance of the Linked Release Test, you're ready to take the Graduate Course. The graduate chapters will apply the technique you've learned through the Undergraduate Course to specific conditions and performance. As you read through the graduate chapters, if you're not confident with the techniques presented, look back at the appropriate chapter in the Undergraduate Course and practice again on easier terrain if needed.

Chapter 11:

Carving

What can be said about carving that hasn't already been repeated, plagiarized or trivialized? According to comments posted on the German Amazon Web site by a reviewer of my first book, "Finally, a simple approach to carving that can be learned by all skiers." I think that just about sums up what we teach in PMTS. We regard carving to be the standard for basic turns, although carving seems to be considered an elusive goal by many skiers. Carving has many faces and can mean different things to different skiers. In some circles, carving has grown into an almost separate sport within skiing, just as bump and mogul competitions are not mainstream skiing, and driving contests are not really golf games for the average player. Bump skiing is still fun and a long drive off the tee is a thrill.

PMTS Direct Parallel defines its turns as consistent with carved turns. The principles of sound parallel skiing should be based on carving. Some say that PMTS puts too much emphasis on carving. I think that those who believe carving isn't the whole game see it as a one-application turn with specific technique. I see carving, through the application of the accurate biomechanics in PMTS, as the ultimate expression of using shaped skis as they are designed. When I ski bumps or powder, I use the basic PMTS movements with minor modifications. When I carve, I use the same PMTS movements, but with appropriate tuning for the snow surface and ski design. I don't use a completely different technique, as many would suggest is required.

This isn't a new controversy, but PMTS Direct Parallel has rekindled the flames and added a new wrinkle. Carving has been in dispute since the 1970s when Warren Witherell basically threw down the gauntlet and insinuated that racers carve and instructors skid and teach skidding. I know

Warren well and contributed to his book *The Athletic Skier*. I think most of his initial assertion is still valid. It isn't surprising that some ski technicians and theorists believe that learning to ski with carving movements limits skiing development. I think this point of view is prevalent because they believe that carving requires specialized technique and movements. I agree that, compared to traditional movements, carving is a new and different technique, but I disagree with the idea that carving limits a skier's potential. Unfortunately for skiers, this position has restricted development of skiing techniques for shaped skis on a global scale. PMTS is a different viewpoint: it demonstrates that biomechanically efficient movements can be versatile enough to include carving as well as mild brushing.

A Moderate Speed Carved Turn

PMTS technique and movements are the same at the basic level as at the uppermost expert levels. The distinction between the levels is the intensity and speed of movement. Quicker reactions are needed when skiing faster and on steeper terrain. The following photo sequence introduces carved turns on blue level (intermediate) terrain. The only difference between this moderate carved turn and a high-level, high-speed turn on steep slopes is the reduced dynamics that result from lower speed and slope angle.

Pure carving usually results in wider and larger turns at first, as you want the skis to produce the arc. With pure carving the turn radius is dependent on side cut, ski bend and ski angle. A carving novice will not know immediately how to bend the ski or increase the edge angle. It is necessary to learn both if you want to carve at high speed with large edge and body angles.

The radius of a carved turn can be reduced (the arc tightened) by increasing pressure on the ski. Think of a bow and arrow: as you pull the arrow back further, the bend of the bow increases. The arm supporting the bow can be compared to the outside leg in a carved turn. When you extend the leg in a carved turn, you bow the ski. The tighter bow of the ski creates a tighter turn as the ski edge bites into the snow and the ski slices along that edge. Tipping the ski to a greater edge angle also tightens the turn arc by pressing the wide ski tip and tail into the snow. The wider tip and tail bite into the snow more than the narrow waist, so again the ski bends into a tighter bow.

In the days of traditional skis, when the side cuts were almost nonexistent and the sides of a ski were virtually parallel, it took a great deal of pressure to the forward part of the ski to make the tip dig in. In those days technique was dictated by ski design. Expert skiers of that era had the capability to "get forward" far enough to bend the tip and begin carving the ski. Intermediates were taught to twist the skis because it was believed that they didn't have the strength or technique for the expert's forward move. Shaped skis don't require nearly that forward pressure to bring about a carved turn; therefore, more skiers can learn to ski like experts. As I have demonstrated a number of times, the old method not only won't be needed, it actually overpowers the shaped ski, making the tail wash out. Let's look at the photos on the next pages and learn the new way to carve.

Fig. 11-1. *Carved turn at moderate speed*

Cues for Success

- Tip the inside ski onto its outside edge.
- In transition, relax the legs so your body moves downhill across your skis as they flatten.
- Show your back to the inside of the turn.

Fig. a. You're still in the turn, prior to transition. Keep your outside leg almost straight, and your inside ski light and tipped. Your lateral balance should be solidly on your outside ski.

Fig. b. The turn is almost complete. Begin to swing the pole, slightly relax and flex the legs.

Fig. c. Flexing the legs flattens your ski angle, and starts your knees and body moving downhill over the skis.

Fig. d. As you relax and flatten further, your body's momentum directs your center downhill over your skis. Balance now on both skis – the float.

Fig. e. Tip your lower ski onto its outside edge to draw the uphill ski onto its big-toe edge. Your legs will follow the tipping actions. Only use tipping movements of the feet, as steering or turning the legs or rotating the upper body will eliminate your balance and therefore also the carving.

Fig. f. Here is where you start to use the movements of Chapter 10, "Upper and Lower Body Coordination." As the turn progresses, bring your inside arm forward and hold your uphill hip back. You may think of the movements as "showing your back" to the inside of the turn.

Fig. g. Here, the relationship between your upper and lower body should resemble that in the straight line ULBC exercise, *Figures 10-15* and *10-16*. Here, with speed, you will be much more angled to the snow, toward the center of the turn.

Fig. h. Continue tipping the inside ski, controlling the upper body. Not much is effort is required — just let the ski do its job.

Fig. i. Tip the free ski further onto its outside edge to increase your body angle. The inside ski can touch the snow, but you should keep it light. If you are able to lift it slightly from the snow, then you are skiing in balance. As you approach the bottom of the turn, let your shoulders and hips start to turn with the skis, as in *Figure a*. Bringing the upper body to square off or turn with the skis at the end of the turn is a natural progression of a completed, round turn and preparation for the next turn.

Carving and PMTS Movements

You may realize that the first skiing movements you were taught didn't include parallel carving ability. Traditionally, conventional teaching tries to minimize and trivialize the importance of carving. Some try to suggest that PMTS teaches an aggressive version of a carving turn too early in the learning process. I agree that beginning skiers with the ability only to rail their skis down the beginner slope using the side cut of the ski are dangerous to themselves and others, but this isn't what happens with skiers who learn PMTS. On the contrary, most skiers learning PMTS learn a brushed carve and brushed direction change. The great advantage of PMTS is that it is designed to quickly bring a skier who is ready up to the level of a carved turn.

If a skier has a natural tendency to rail the ski, which, incidentally, is not carving, de-tuning this to a brushed carve turn is a natural outcome of the PMTS process. We also differentiate between a skidded turn and a brushed carve. We do not teach skidding; we teach movements that create ski and speed control. A brushed carve is a turn with a slightly less aggressive edge angle in the snow that produces a wider track. You will probably acquire that turn through PMTS before you learn the complete locked carved turn. When learning a carved turn, the aggressive skier should be able to leave two clean, single, narrow tracks in the snow, while the less aggressive skier produces a mildly brushed turn. Neither of these turns conflicts with the ski's design. Skidding does! If you find yourself using different techniques to carve or skid your turns, or to make long or short turns, you haven't learned the right technique yet.

It is probably obvious by now that the fundamental movements of PMTS will enable you to ski using parallel carving. Those who want to achieve a higher level, such as skiing at high edge angles with pronounced body angle, will have to work with greater concentration on these skills. If you apply everything you learned in the Undergraduate Course, you will be able to carve just as Diana and I demonstrate in the photos. The technique doesn't change. The timing and movements are described in detail with the photos.

Fig. 11-2. *Roles of inside and outside leg in carved turn*

> **Cues for Success**
>
> • Flex the inside leg and tip that ski on its outside edge.
>
> • Keep the outside leg extended and the ski pressured while you balance on it.

Fig. a. Carved turns at a high edge angle and body angle result from the dynamic version of movements described in the previous photo series. Strongly flexing your inside leg and tipping your inside ski allow you to tip to this angle.

Fig. b. This position is almost the same, but it is further along in the turn. Continue to tip the inside ski onto its little-toe edge. Flexing your inside leg while you tip that ski enables your body to move closer to the snow, further inside the turn. As you flex the inside leg, keep the outside leg extended. Many skiers believe that the body is being pushed into the turn by the extension of the outside leg. This is not the case, and attempting to do so likely will make you lose your balance.

Fig. c. Keep strong muscle tension in the outside leg to resist the forces and to bend the outside ski. Doing so will store energy in the bent ski. When you flex to release, the stored energy will propel you into the new turn.

Equipment for Carving

A number of the Alpine nations of Europe host carving competitions based on skiing around cones, like water skiers in a slalom. They use techniques that are defined by a wide stance and very specialized equipment. In contrast, the photos you see in this book are taken using basic skis and normal equipment. Carving competitors use very short, narrow-waisted skis, with very high lifters under the binding and boots. They don't use poles and they reach their arms out to the snow to keep from falling over. Most of the skiers in such competitions use upper-body rotation to bring the skis around more quickly. As you can see, this form of skiing is very specialized — not a method for everyday use.

Ski racers also carve because it is the best way to maintain speed and control. They have more disciplined upper-body movements than those in the carving competitions, but they do use specialized equipment.

What can we aspire to in carving? We have to take equipment into consideration. I had a number of clients last year who had great difficulty learning to carve on wide-waisted all-mountain and "free riding" skis. When used for what they are designed to do, they're good skis, and skiers who can already carve may be able to do so on these skis. However, they aren't carving skis, and the salesperson should let you know that when you buy them.

As mentioned above, the photos in this section of the book are taken of skiers using normal equipment that anyone can buy. I don't like to provide too much information about specific equipment models within company lines, as after a year many of the models no longer exist, and after two years improved technology is usually available. In my case, the skis I am shown using are Elan Hyper Carves. The Hyper Carves can be skied in the bumps or in all-mountain conditions; however, they have an aggressive shape, a side cut that generates a turn radius of approximately 14 meters. Skis like this are made by all major companies and should be available for a number of years to come. Head has the Cyber Slalom Ti and the Cyber X-60, for example, and Atomic has the BetaCarve 9.14 and the even more aggressive 9.11. I recommend any of these skis for a carving fan, and especially for the skier who aspires to learn carving.

To the Realm of High-Angle Carving

What will take us beyond regular carved turns and let us achieve high-angled carved turns? Remember the section in the introduction about not turning your skis? If ever there was a situation in which trying to turn your skis will eliminate success, it is in carving. Only movements that change edge angles and tipping actions that move across the skis at 90 degrees to the direction of travel produce success. In the upper- and lower-body coordination ("ULBC") section of the Undergraduate Course, you will find the basics for lateral movements required for high-angled carved turns. The slope doesn't have to be steep! In fact, a moderate slope is better to learn on. The photos for this book were all taken on blue terrain. Intensive and aggressive movements are required to develop high angles in turns. Your allies in this endeavor are the skis' side cut and the greater momentum that develops as you pick up speed and engage the skis. Literally, you let the ski do the turning. This may sound too simplistic, but it couldn't be easier.

Fig. 11-3. Set up the angles, then refine your balance

Fig. a. Diana demonstrates a powerful early angle in this turn. A perfect release from the previous turn helps you achieve this early and extreme body angle. It lets the energy from the previous turn launch you into this position in the new turn.

Fig. b. Tighten the arc further by flexing the inside leg and tipping the inside ski further

Fig. c. Now it's just a matter of maintaining balance. Often you can refine and improve your balance on the stance ski with subtle changes to the inside "strong arm" position; fine adjustments such as lifting or lowering. Use simple movements such as tipping and flexing to establish the turn, and then focus on maintaining balance with small adjustments.

Fig. d. The turn is almost over. Start to relax your leg muscles, giving in to the turning forces that will take your body over your skis into the next turn.

Cues for Success

- A good release sets up early turn angles.
- Fine tune your balance with your inside "strong arm."

Fig. 11-4. Tighten the arc by tipping the inside foot

Fig. a. Diana demonstrates the dynamics of a carved turn with balance on the outside ski and strong flexion and tipping of the inside leg.

Fig. b. Increase the body angle and tighten the turn radius by tipping your inside ski further. This is evidenced by the external rotation of Diana's inside femur. Ski angles are identical. This extremely dynamic skiing cannot be accomplished with the "skis-apart-weight-on-both-feet" school of carving. Keep the inside boot touching the outside leg. As you flex the inside leg, draw it up along the outside leg. You'll increase the vertical distance between your feet — not the horizontal distance — making it easier to maintain balance on the outside ski. During the release, as your leg length evens out, your skis will once again be side-by-side.

Cues for Success

- Tip the inside ski onto its outside edge far enough that the inside thigh moves outward.
- Keep the inside foot along the outside leg.

Fig. 11-5. Tighten the arc by flexing the inside leg

Cues for Success

• Tip the inside ski and shorten that leg to pull your body into the turn.

• Keep the free, inside foot in contact with the outside leg.

Fig. a. Again, flex the inside leg and tip the inside ski to draw your body down into the center of the turn.

Fig. b. Increase tipping and flexing with the inside leg to tighten the radius and give you a tighter turn than what the side cut alone would yield. Again, keep your inside foot in contact with the outside leg throughout the tipping and flexing.

Relax the Stance Leg to "Use the Force"

As with everything simple, some background information may help. What I presented in the ULBC section of the book is still applicable. Balance is the key to carving, as it is to most other things in correct skiing. If you can change the direction of your skis by tipping the skis and leaving two thin lines in the snow, then you have the basic skills necessary for learning high-angle carving.

The next thing that you must add to your repertoire is leg retraction, or flexion. This is just what we covered in Chapter 7, "Use the Force." At the precise moment that the ski tips start to head back across the fall line at the bottom of the turn, you must flex your stance leg aggressively. Flexing is the opposite of pushing off the ski. It means shortening your leg under control so your body center moves closer to the ski. In almost every turn in this book, you will see that at the turn transition, the skier's body is moving closer to the ski at the release. We have discussed how this is accomplished numerous times. Relaxing the stance leg begins the release, but in carving you want to use the energy from one turn to take you into the next. The timing and speed of the transition become very important. If you are too late, you cannot take advantage of your body's optimal momentum in the direction of the new turn. Quickly flexing your leg will move your center closer to the ski and bring your skis flat to the snow. If, at the same time, you add the elements of the Weighted Release, the transition is even faster.

Review, if needed, the elements of the Weighted Release in the Undergraduate Course. Keeping your weight on the stance ski as you relax to release literally can propel you into the next turn.

Fig. 11-6. Control the relaxation of your stance leg

Fig. a. Coming out of the turn requires a relaxation of the leg muscles and fine control of the rate of flattening. Here I'm just beginning to relax.

Fig. b. Just a slight relaxation of your stance leg muscles will bring your body back over your skis. Maintain balance on your outside ski until it is completely flat on the snow, then lighten it and tip it on its outside edge so it becomes the inside ski for the new turn.

Cues for Success

- Control your rate of relaxing and flattening.
- Balance on your outside ski until it is completely flat on the snow.

Fig. 11-7. Time your release for a quick transition

Fig. a. Lead the tipping actions with the inside ski to draw the outside ski on edge at an equal edge angle. Keep your outside leg long so the inside ski tipping will pull your body far inside the turn.

Fig. b. Begin to relax the legs – they'll flex more (shorten), your body will start to move downhill over the skis, and the skis will start to flatten to the snow.

Fig. c. The turn is complete – let the turn forces pull your body into the new turn. Notice how quickly the skis and body change angles from one turn to the next.

Fig. d. Committing to the next turn is easy if you keep the inside ski light at the beginning so the body can be pulled into the center of the turn.

Fig. e. Early body angle in the turn is possible when the inside ski doesn't interfere with letting the body drop into the turn. If you place too much weight on the inside ski, it will stop your body from moving into the turn. The body and ski angles are blocked from increasing, and the speed and carving energy is lost.

Fig. f. Let your inside ski skim over the surface, ready to increase tipping angle.

Cues for Success

- Keep the outside leg long until the last 3/4 of the turn.
- Keep the inside ski light, just skimming the snow.

Chapter 12:

Bumps

Bumps or mogul competence is considered a milestone or rite of passage to expert skiing. A standard we often set for our skiers at the Loveland Ski Area in Colorado is to ski the whole Avalanche Bowl (rated double black diamond) without traversing or stopping. You are on your way to becoming an expert when you can meet this challenge. I have assembled many examples of skiing steep bumps at high speed in order to highlight the different skills needed and to help you achieve this level of skiing. If you have already developed the basics for short turns, you have the essentials to master bump skiing. It goes without saying that a solid short turn with a strong pole plant is a necessity. I'm not saying you can't ski in the bumps without those abilities, but you will not ski like an expert. You'll get down, but you'll struggle. It will take you a long time to feel confident without a command of the basics introduced in the Undergraduate Course, if you ever are able to achieve that confidence. The essential components for bumps or mogul competence are listed in order:

1. short turn
2. pole plant
3. upper- and lower-body coordination

If you learned to use the movements in the previous sections and are comfortable with the techniques presented, you're ready to start the graduate bump course that follows.

Strong young skiers may decide to skip the Undergraduate Course in the first section of the book because they believe they can learn by doing. Many readers of my first book confessed to me that they made that error in judgment. They told me that after looking through my book and selecting what they wanted to learn from the many photographs and montages, they turned right to their favorite sections. They immediately went out on the slopes and tried the movements. Fortunately, most of them were successful, in spite of incomplete background preparation. Only later did they read the whole book. They confessed that after going through the whole book, they gained a greater understanding of how to use my system and were rewarded with even greater improvements. It is human nature to reach for instant success and read the most intriguing part of the book first. Some of you may be reading this section before any other.

If you find that this chapter produces immediate results for you with a direct approach, I can't keep you from trying it. But if you find you are having some difficulties, go back and read the introduction and study the Undergraduate Course; it will make a difference.

Without the fundamental movements introduced earlier in the book you may develop a defensive bump-skiing technique. Another downside of improvised bump skiing is the physical grind and the beating your legs will take. When the new shaped skis came out, I realized that I had been avoiding bumps on my 204 cm slalom skis. The new skis opened the door for me. Traditional skis, with their lack of side cut and enormous length, required considerable effort to wiggle through a steep bump field. All that leg torquing and ski bending takes power and strength. If you have a weak link like I do — a bad knee — it can be very painful. Bump skiing can be experienced with less pounding and impact by using efficient movements. Extraneous movements take time and energy; expert bump skiing doesn't have room for these inefficiencies. I use the primary movements exactly as explained in the beginning photos and montages of this Graduate Course.

Control and graceful movement with flair and energy are my goals for bump skiing. Scary, uncontrolled airtime and physical beatings are not my idea of sophisticated bump skiing. Timing your turn to take advantage of the bump's shape and contour is an important part of tactical bump skiing. Before you can use a well-synchronized release that matches a bump's contours, your movements must be ingrained and rehearsed. One of the benefits of learning PMTS is that you can make the movements as quickly or as slowly as you wish to control speed.

Line or Timing of Movements in Bumps

Achieving a line in the bumps is similar to trying to stay on line in a racecourse. If you haven't developed the movement capabilities to stay with a line yet, all coaching and descriptions won't get you there. I frequently see a lot of fuss being made about line. It's putting the cart before the horse. You can't control where you are going unless you have the technique to get there. Just as steering and skidding your skis won't keep you on the ideal line through a racecourse, these techniques won't keep you fluid and in control through the bumps. Learn the proper technique, and you will be successful in the racecourse and with picking your turns in the bumps.

The fastest way to find the ideal line through the bumps is by using correct movements at the top, on the other side, going down and in the hollow between bumps. If you use the series of movements developed in PMTS you will be able to

- engage by tilting the inside ski at the top of the bump.
- let the outside ski come to an edge on the front face of the bump.
- increase edge angle by tipping the inside ski through the turn and extending the outside leg to stay in contact with the snow.

Use these prescribed movements, and the outside leg will be extended, and the ski will be change directions. By the time you approach the hollow between bumps, you will be in balance and in the perfect position to flex the extended outside leg which will absorb the hollow and bump lip while releasing the skis for the next turn.

Rarely do we have much choice about what we are facing next in fast, steep bumps. Choosing the ideal line in bumps is more a reaction to the bump directly in front rather than an established line you have chosen. Bump skiing is a game of reactions. Looking ahead to the next bump, after you have figured what to do for the one you are in, is the answer. Just because racers study the course doesn't mean they are always picking the line they will ski. In fact, the truly great racers study the general contours and direction of the course, but they make adjustments on the course to gain more speed. If you are planning for an ideal line, you may be restricting your freedom and be late with your movements. A racer — and I have known a few who prepare in this manner — who is overly concerned about exactly where to be on every gate usually will have a slow run. Looking ahead to the next gate and using accurate movements that bring the skis to the best arc is a successful tactic.

Rarely is a bump run as uniform as a racecourse. If you deviate slightly on a racecourse you can get back on line within a gate or two. If you deviate on a bump run from an intended line you will run into a completely new configuration of bumps. A true bump skier is versatile and adaptable, ready for any change in terrain.

If you are new to bumps, start your preparation on intermediate bump runs. Try connecting two or three bumps at a time. In this case, you can see far enough down the slope to plan a line. Develop your turning by tipping just as in all levels of PMTS. When you can bring the short turn movements practiced earlier into the bump, you will find the success you are looking for. The description of bump skiing at this expert level completely applies to bump skiing at the introductory level; only the terrain changes.

Foot Speed

One of the essential capabilities for bump skiing is foot speed. You may ask, "what is foot speed? It sounds important, and I think I'd like it, but what does it mean?" I asked that question when I first heard about foot speed in skiing. Does it mean I must move my feet more quickly? I thought runners or tennis players needed that ability, not skiers. In fact, many of the great skiers I coached had slow feet and ran poorly. Again, I think this term stems from the visual impression of skiers who are changing direction very quickly. It does make sense because all the movements associated with changing direction involve the feet and skis. To the untrained eye, it looks as though great skiers move their feet very quickly. Not just any quick foot movements will do; being quick with a selected set of movements is the key to bumping without thumping.

Fig. 12-1. *The basics in bumps*

Figures 12-1 and *12-2* are the same turn. *Figure 12-1* has been expanded so you can see the actions in the individual frames. *Figure 12-2* shows you the actual placement of the turn in the moguls. These bumps are big and tight on a steep hill, and the turns are very short and quick.

Fig. a. Plant the pole and begin the release.
Fig. b. Hold onto the pole for stability. Let the skis float, avoiding any urge to twist them. Begin tipping and rolling the inside ski strongly to its new edge.
Fig. c. Keep the inside hand moving forward after you have passed the pole to keep your upper body lined across the fall line. After the float phase, the body is back in balance over the skis.
Fig. d. Swing the pole tip for the next pole plant.
Fig. e. Plant the pole and allow the skis to float.
Fig. f. Push the inside hand forward while preparing the other hand for the new swing. Always keep the pole plant movements going. One pole or the other should be swinging to a plant at all times.

Fig. 12-2. Use the release to generate foot speed

Fig. a. As the skis float (run straight and flat for the briefest moment), pull the lower ski back under your body while tilting it toward the outside edge.

Fig. b. Tilt the new inside ski until its outside edge touches the snow. Continue tilting and flexing to bring the skis around the bump.

Fig. c. The next release has redirected the skis to point downhill. Finish the turn by tilting the free foot strongly and pressing it against the stance ski.

The movements you must learn in order to improve your direction change in the bumps are the release and balance shift, or transfer. If you start a new turn without re-establishing your balance, you are in for an uncomfortable thumping. Shifting your balance from one side, or foot, to the other is the key movement for successful bump skiing. So you always need to prepare to shift your balance for the next turn. Balance results from having a solid platform. Releasing shifts your body, establishing a new stance foot, but tipping engages the stance ski, creating a solid platform with the new stance foot.

Weighting the Skis

To purists, weighting or unweighting technically may be the wrong words to describe functional skiing actions. But when I ski, I can feel pressure building under my foot as I increase the push against the ski by extending my leg. I also can feel more pressure as my ski tips to a greater angle to the snow. The feeling of increased pressure or weight under my ski or foot indicates to me that my body is changing position or shifting in response to the forces of the terrain. Pressure can be sensed and described by skiers in many ways; weight shift is one of these ways. When we use efficient movements, the body naturally will move to balance over the new stance ski or foot. The body responds to the changing forces by aligning itself over the ski to stay in balance. As I release from the downhill edge of the previous turn, my stance ski becomes my free foot. My balance shifts to the new stance ski and I create contact with that ski by extending the leg. This is the switch in pressure to the new weighted, downhill side of my body. The former downhill side of the body is now the less weighted, or free, side. The free side should continue tipping to engage the ski, and is able to make movements that improve and maintain balance. Most of these explanations are descriptions of how the body should behave and react. These examples are different from external cues. However, sometimes an explanation of this kind creates additional insight for skiers and offers another way to understand the techniques in addition to those developed solely through the use of effective external cues.

Earlier in the book I wrote that the primary purpose of technique should be to create balance. I prefer to limit the use of technical explanations and references such as "weight shifting" or "pressure shift" because they become too technical. Using the idea of transferring balance makes more sense. If you transfer balance you have no choice but to shift pressure and weight, and as they shift, balance is re-established. The big advantage of thinking about transferring balance is that you produce the appropriate amount of edge angle, body alignment and pressuring in the right place, every time. Think about balance first and you will do only what you have to do to achieve balance. This method is an economical way to move and a first-class way to develop consistency. I like to use simple movements and get results by focusing on cues that combine many actions. This approach gives the skier less to think about and produces superb results.

Fig. 12-3. Chris Anthony demonstrates the actions of the free foot

Fig. a. Flex the legs to absorb the bottom of the turn. Let the skis float, and hold firmly to the planted pole.
Fig. b. Still holding the pole, flex the inside leg and tip it to the outside edge.
Fig. c. Tipping the inside ski redirects the skis, as in a release.
Fig. d. Extend the outside leg to reach for the surface and prepare the pole plant.
Fig. e. Flex the legs and absorb the transition.
Fig. f. Let the skis float, but focus on pulling the inside ski back.
Fig. g. Pulling the skis back causes the skis to match the angle of the slope for the next turn.

Revisit the Phantom Move

We come back to the Phantom Move to demonstrate how one simple action begins a chain reaction of movements for the whole body. The Phantom Move sounds almost too simple to work, but it is effective beyond expectations. I love to hear comments about the Phantom Move from the traditional ski-teaching community, which criticizes PMTS as a system that has only one move, not believing that something so simple can work so well.

PMTS is a complete system, not a "single move." The criticism shows a lack of understanding about PMTS, but I take those comments as compliments. If you can ski like an expert by thinking about only one movement, what a great achievement! When you break the Phantom Move into smaller parts, it can become very complex. As with many simple concepts, there is complex reasoning behind it. In this case, skiing does become rocket science, but you don't have to know the science to ski it — that's the beauty of PMTS. The Phantom Move is much more than one move; it sets into action a chain or series of efficient movements.

When skiers analyze the Phantom Move, they find they are actually performing the following movements:

- releasing the skis by flattening the angle of the outside or stance ski;
- transferring to the new outside ski by lightening or lifting the previous outside ski, making it the free ski or the new inside ski;
- engaging by tilting or tipping the inside ski to the little-toe or outside edge and continuing to tip that ski through the finish of the turn.

This description is a complete breakdown of the actions of a Phantom Move. The Phantom Move makes it possible to get out of a turn, move the body directly into balance over the new outside ski, engage the skis on their new set of edges and continue completing the turn. A simple description of performing the Phantom Move is to lighten the old downhill ski and tip or tilt it toward its outside edge. Once you learn this sequence of movements, your lower-body focus can be the Phantom Move.

In *Figure 12-4*, Chris Anthony, Alaska Extreme Champion and veteran World Extreme Championship competitor, demonstrates a direct line in a steep bump run. He is very quick from one transition to the other, performing linked Phantom Moves. The critical time in these turns is after the release. The transfer and engagement must be performed early in the turn so balance is maintained. Notice how early Chris uses his free foot to set up the ski and body angles. The beauty of the Phantom Move is that one move can influence the whole turn set-up, which is the biomechanical advantage of using PMTS in the bumps.

Biomechanical Advantage

- When the stance ski turns as a result of free-foot tipping, you are able to extend the stance leg rather than twisting it. You maintain snow contact, and get the full range of flexion to absorb the crest of the upcoming bump.

g *f* *e* *d*

Fig. a. Here at the end of the turn is the last moment your edges are gripping. Swing the pole basket forward to prepare for the pole plant.

Fig. b. Relax the legs and let the skis flatten and float.

Fig. c. Gather in your releasing foot — now the free foot — by lifting and pulling it in toward the stance foot.

Fig. d. As the free foot comes in to match the stance foot, tip it toward the outside edge. Notice how much direction change is accomplished.

Fig. e. The next pole plant stabilizes the upper body and coordinates with the release.

Fig. f. Chris releases the edges and lets the skis float. He prepares the downhill ski to be pulled back and tipped for the next turn.

Fig. g. His free foot's tipping and pulling-in actions have set him up perfectly for the next turn.

> **Cues for Success**
>
> • Pull the previous downhill ski and boot in to touch and hold against the new stance ski.
>
> • Pull the free foot in prior to the next hollow.

c *b* *a*

Fig. 12-4. Linked Phantom Moves directly in the fall line

Connected Phantom Moves allow very quick edge changes and therefore quick direction changes or turns. Quick feet are important to bump skiing, but how do we achieve them? Quick feet result from a quick relaxation to create a release and a quick pick-up of the ski; actions that are specific to bump skiing. These movements begin the chain reaction I talked about earlier, enabling the body to align with the forces of the next turn. But if we try to think about all the movements that need to happen in a turn transition, we'd never get to the next turn. If we focus on the bare essentials of the Phantom Move, the lift and tip, the deed is done. Technically speaking, it isn't just the feet that must be moved to make quick direction changes. The muscles of the upper and medial side of the leg, hip and lower back all contribute and are recruited. All the mechanisms are put into place and activated without conscious thought. Keep your mind as clear as possible; simplify. Develop your ability to move in the bumps by learning to link Phantom Moves.

Wrist Management

Diana demonstrates superb timing and wrist management in this steep bump run. Early pole preparation is a mainstay of expert bump skiing. You need to feel that your pole plant is part of your support system in the bumps.

Going into gravitational games without a stabilizing pole plant is like showing up at a gunfight without a gun. You're just not going to be in the game. Study the upper and lower body coordination section of this book before you ski bumps. The photos and captions here explain and demonstrate the importance of the stabilizing pole plant.

Cues for Success

- Keep the pole in contact with the snow long enough to use it.
- After the pole is released, bring your hands and arms back to Home Base.
- Swing the outside pole early to prepare for the upcoming turn.

Fig. 12-5. Using a stabilizing pole plant in bumps

Fig. a. Diana prepares to absorb and change direction for the next bump.
Fig. b. The pole is planted and the legs are relaxed and flexed to absorb the bump.
Fig. c. Diana lets the skis float out from under her body in an aggressive manner but keeps them in control with a strong free foot pull-back and tipping movement. The pulling back of the free foot results in the tip-down position of the free ski.
Fig. d. The results are perfect. As soon as her skis redirect from the release and tipping, her body has caught up and she is in perfect balance. Her outside leg is extended, maintaining contact and preparing for flexion.
Fig. e. She extends the legs to be able to absorb the next bump.
Fig. f. She keeps the movements going with another early preparation of the pole swing for the upcoming bump.

The Pole is Another Point of Contact

A strong pole plant is paramount for successful expert bump skiing. As you learned in Chapter 10, "Upper and Lower Body Coordination," the pole swing and timing must be in synch with the turn and release. Here is the plant and release example.

Skiing with a correct pole plant is like manually shifting gears in a car while turning the steering wheel to match the curve. Millions of drivers have learned to drive a manual transmission and sports car buyers still demand a stick shift. If all these drivers can accomplish this feat, skiers can learn how to use a stabilizing pole plant for the bumps.

Fig. 12-6. Plant the pole for an additional point of contact

Fig. a. Complete your turn with a strong, stabilizing pole plant.
Fig. b. Flatten both skis and allow them to float out from under your body. The pole still is strongly planted for added support.

Biomechanical Advantage

- Flattening the skis uncoils the strong upper-to-lower-body counteraction of the previous turn.

Float with Foot Retraction

Sometimes you must absorb sharp bumps that you know will launch you airborne otherwise. The best thing to do is stop tipping, relax the legs and flex the knees quickly. You will be in a seated position coming over the other side of the bump as in *Figure 12-7b* (following page). The benefit of this unweighted or lightly weighted situation is that it makes the skis easy to manage. While the skis are still light, organize the free foot for the next turn. While extending the outside leg to make contact with the hollow of the next bump, pull the free foot in toward the stance boot and back under the body. These movements will bring you over your skis and in balance for the turn finish.

Recovering balance in bump skiing requires that the free foot be pulled back strongly in the transition between turns. I first started pulling the free foot back 20 years ago because, like all racers, I was often getting caught "in the back seat" — racer terminology for being too far behind your skis. Racers normally don't park, or camp out, in the back seat; they usually find themselves stranded there as their feet and skis accelerate forward without warning. You may have experienced this sensation. Out of nowhere in an aggressive turn, your skis lock onto an edge and they jet forward, leaving you sitting back with your legs levered against the back of your boots, out of control and hanging on for dear life. Skiers whose normal stance tends to be on the verge of leaning back find themselves in this situation more often. Losing your feet like that is a frightening experience and can have long-term effects on your confidence. If you are skiing in fear of another occurrence, it could severely hamper your progress and dampen your enthusiasm for all-mountain skiing.

The only solution for this problem was to instruct skiers to lean forward or place their shins on the front of the boots. Other frequently heard recommendations were to stand up more, flex your boots more, lift your rear, project your hips forward, or hold your hands in front of you. Unfortunately, none of these recommendations is adequate. The fastest and most effective way to get yourself recentered fore/aft over your skis is to move your base of support back. Moving your foot back has the effect of moving your hips forward. How should you get the skis back? Generally in skiing, your weight or pressure is on the downhill, or outside ski, making this ski very hard to move once it is set on edge. Skis that are floating, or unweighted, in the transition between turns are easy to control and move. In the short turn section of the Undergraduate Course, I introduced pulling the free foot back as one of the basic necessities for all-mountain skiing. Now you can apply it to bumps.

a

Fig. a. When there is a sharp kicker, as on this bump, be ready to flex by bringing your knees up to your chest and letting the skis float.

b

Fig. b. Balance on the pole while you organize the tilting movements of the free foot.

c

Fig. c. Tilting the inside foot, bringing it against the stance foot and extending the outside leg have brought my body back over my feet.

d

Fig. d. Increase the flex of the inside leg and tilting of that ski to make a sharper turn.

Fig. e-f. Relax and flex both legs to suck up the bump.

f

e

Fig. 12-7. Retract the free foot to stay centered in bumps

Cues for Success

- Organize the free foot while the skis are light or floating.

Extend the Legs After the Release

Fig. 12-8. *Extend the legs after release to have a full range of flexion*

Fig. a. Reach out with the legs to make contact after the bump.
Fig. b. Flex the legs to absorb the bump.
Fig. c. Plant the pole for balance and to time the release. Let the skis float between turns.
Fig. d. While floating, tip the inside ski (the previous stance ski) to prepare for the direction change. Pull and hold that ski back to produce a balanced stance for the turn.
Fig. e. Notice how Chris is organized with both skis at the same angle, feet close together both fore/aft and laterally, and legs extended to absorb the hollow of the next bump.

At the point in the turn at which you are ready to release your edges, focus on the lower or downhill ski. Your pole should be firmly planted in the snow, as in *Figure c*. Your skis should be flat at or just before the crown of the bump. As your ski tips become free of the snow and stick out over the bump, tip the new inside ski or free foot to the outside edge and pull that boot back under your hips, as in *Figure d*. These two movements can be accomplished simultaneously. Pull the heel of the free foot back. This is the move that will keep you in balance and turning, make your bump skiing successful. The contour of the bumps makes this move extremely important. After you drop off the top of the bump to its front side, the face of the bump becomes much steeper. If you are skiing fast, the lip of the bump tends to launch you. Stay calm, use your pole and free foot, and you will land in balance, headed in the right direction.

Cues for Success

- Flex the inside leg more than the outside.
- Press the free foot against the outside boot.

Pull the Free Ski Back to Drop the Tips

Diana comes into an abrupt transition with speed. She has her work cut out for her to avoid getting launched off the bump. She sucks her knees up quickly and tips her previous downhill ski to the outside edge. Holding the inside ski back as she crests the bump allows her to change the fore/aft relationship of her upper body to her lower body. Her upper body moves forward and her boots stay under her hips. This is the technique skiers have been searching for to stay balanced over their skis in the bumps. No amount of hip thrusting or knee driving will achieve this re-centering. Use the biomechanical advantage that Diana demonstrates here – pull your free foot back to stay centered.

A well-prepared bump skier will simply pull the free foot back and therefore be able to drop the tips to match the steep contour on the front side of the bump. All the components of the Undergraduate Course are applied at this moment. If you omit any one of them, your likelihood of success drops dramatically. The pole plant must be solid as demonstrated by the accompanying photos. The free foot must be held back and tipped to match the stance ski angle. Although it seems like the skis are too far ahead of the body after the release, this situation is quickly rectified when the skis react to the tipping actions initiated in the release. Your skis will float if you release at the right time: that is, at the very transition or crown of the bump. This is the time to initiate a strong backward pulling action by the free foot, while at the same time tipping the ski. Study the photos that accompany this section and practice this movement in easy terrain before you try it in the bumps.

a

b

c

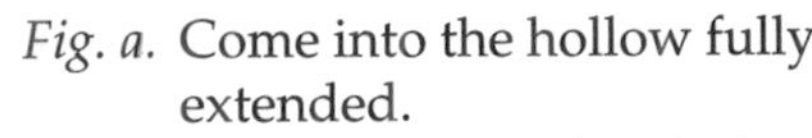

Fig. a. Come into the hollow fully extended.
Fig. b. Flex the legs to absorb the transition.
Fig. c. Tip the inside ski and pull it back at the top of the bump to change direction.

Fig. 12-9. Pull the free foot back to drop the ski tips

Biomechanical Advantage

- Pull your free foot back so your body can keep up with your skis.

Keep the Upper Body Facing the Fall Line

a b c d e Fig. 12-10. Keep the upper body facing downhill

In *Figure 12-10* on the previous page, Craig McNeil, a former pro freestyle competitor, shows an athletic, aggressive bump approach.

Fig. a. Craig comes into the hollow fully extended and in balance.
Fig. b. He plants the pole and flexes to absorb the bump.
Fig. c. He goes for good air but his skis are turned, his tips are aimed down to match the steep face of the bump, and his body is already lined up for the next turn.
Fig. d. He is in perfect balance again thanks to his release and the tilting of the inside free ski.
Fig. e. Craig reacts to the release of the last bump by letting his skis float and is ready to tip for the next turn.

Notice that for an instant after the release, the skiers let their skis float ahead of their bodies. As soon as the skis are tipped and the free foot is pulled back and close to the stance boot, matching the ski edge angles, the body catches up and is in balance over the skis once more. The photos were taken on very aggressive, steep bump runs. You might want to start learning this advanced set of movements on more forgiving intermediate bumps. Remember, this is a progression starting with effective short turns. If you first become proficient with these very same movements, described in the Undergraduate Course of the book, your ability to use them in bumps will come much more quickly.

Carving in the Bumps

Most skiers are taught to ski bumps by rotating their legs and twisting their skis at the top of the bumps and sliding down the other side to control speed. This method is limiting and keeps the skier at a very low level. Anyone can learn the methods described and taught here. With these methods you make up your mind. Do you want to be blue level proficient at bumps or an aggressive black level skier as demonstrated here? You won't have any limitations of technique if you use these methods. How expert or aggressive do you want to be? These methods will allow you to make the decision rather then have limitations imposed through improper movements.

Fig. a. The most important moves are right at the top of the bump: plant the pole and then lift the downhill ski to make it your free foot.
Fig. b. Tip the lifted foot to the outside edge. As you lift the foot, the stance support disappears. Your body naturally "falls" to the side of the lifted ski.
Fig. c. Keep the inside ski tucked back and hold it close to the stance ski. Notice how the outside ski is tipped well on edge as a result of the inside foot actions. This is as close as you can get to carving in the bumps. I like to ski bumps with a carving technique as it provides better control and uses the ski – the biomechanical advantage.
Fig. d. Tip the inside ski and stand on the outside ski to move your body inside the turn. Extend the outside leg so you'll have a full range of absorption at the bottom of the bump.
Fig. e. Keep the upper body facing downhill. Use counteracting movements of the hips and the strong inside arm position practiced in Chapter 10.
Fig. f. Relax and allow the bump to flex the knees up into the chest. Let the skis float, pull the downhill ski in and back and tip it over to the outside edge.

Fig. 12-11. Carving in Bumps

Carving in the Bumps – The Actual Line

Fig. 12-12. Montage of previous turn, carving in bumps

This is a montage of the frames from *Figure 12-11*. In this montage, the skier appears in his actual position on the slope, giving you a realistic perspective of how quickly and sharply the turn can be made using tipping and absorbing movements. This is a very aggressive line on a steep slope, but that doesn't mean you need to make huge recoveries. The actions of the free foot and ski are clearly demonstrated. The fastest way to transfer is to lift the inside ski, which is accomplished in the second frame. Hold the free boot close to and pressed against the stance boot as in the ball hold exercise. When you press the boots together, edging and body angles develop quickly and with balance. Notice how by the third frame the outside ski is already on a strong edge. My shaped skis for this run are not radical; these are all-mountain skis, yet I still let the side cut take me around the turn, demonstrating carving in the bumps.

Upper and Lower Body Coordination

The next montage, *Figure 12-13*, is part of the same run but further down the slope. I used strong counteracting movements at the beginning of this turn to help achieve this extreme edge angle. The counteracting movements presented in the Undergraduate Course are very important if you want tight, short arcs on steep bump runs. This turn is an example of the power that countering movements offer to redirect the skis for the next turn. Just as in the wall sit, keep your back up against the imaginary wall behind you up the slope. My upper body is facing down the slope, and my skis are turned fully across the slope. As I flatten my skis, I let them float out from under my hips. My pole is planted firmly in the snow for important added support and upper-body stability. My upper body is almost suspended from the pole as the skis are flattened. Once the skis are flat to the snow, press the inside boot against the stance boot and tip the inside ski toward its outside edge. Notice in the third frame, *Figure c*, the pole is no longer supporting my upper body, and my old downhill ski is no longer gripping; therefore, my body moves to the inside of the turn. It is not free falling as some would call this point in a turn. My outside ski is already edged and gripping the snow, and my outside leg is extended to maintain contact with the snow. My tipping actions earlier in the turn brought the outside ski to the correct edge angle. Some will interpret my turn by saying, "Look at how he rotated his legs to steer his skis." I can state unequivocally that I don't use rotation and leg steering to turn. The turning action is a result of balance on the stance ski and tipping of the free foot. I never think about rotating or steering my legs when I ski. I can't feel or sense my edges or the surface when I focus on steering my skis or legs. Instead, I focus on sensing the edge angles of my skis.

Notice in the photos of this chapter, the release occurs on the lip of the bump. Consequently, most turns are initiated at this point. Tipping the inside ski at the crest creates the direction change of the skis. Avoid trying to turn or steer your skis at the top of bumps. Turning or twisting the skis requires that you flex your legs, which keeps you in a low position. With this approach, you have no extension or absorbing ability for the next bump. The muscles required to steer or turn your skis are most effective when your legs are flexed; therefore, to achieve enough force to turn the skis, your legs must stay flexed. In contrast, tipping the inside ski edges and redirects the skis in an efficient manner, providing superior edge grip and control. If you tip the inside ski rather than steer it, the outside leg extends, allowing you to edge and grip with the body balanced on the gripping edge. High-energy, high-speed bump skiing as in the photos in this chapter, is a game of releasing the skis and letting them float. The PMTS approach to re-centering over your the skis is to use the retracting and tipping actions of the free foot. Trying to stay centered all the time, maintaining the same position over your skis while skiing bumps, is also possible by using the same movements, but only with much less speed and more rounded turns. The runs shown here are for expert bump skiers on steep black diamond bumps. The lines demonstrated here are very direct and close to the fall line. If you are developing your bump technique, use exactly the same movements described here in easy bumps on blue terrain. You will find you will be able to stay balanced over your skis and control your speed.

Fig. 12-13. Strong upper- and lower-body counteracting movements in bumps

Cues for Success

- Keep your back square to the fall line.
- Tip the new inside ski first.

Long Legs, Short Legs

Fig. a. John Clendenin, former World Freestyle Champion, demonstrates a rounder line with larger turns. He has time to completely extend the legs between turns.

Fig. b. John relaxes and flexes to absorb the bumps just as we do in the more direct line sequences.

Fig. c. John's early inside foot tipping allows him to be well positioned and already edged, coming down the front side of the bump.

Fig. d. Increased tipping brings the skis across the hill and in position to absorb the next bump.

Fig. 12-14. Full extension and flexion of the legs

Keys for Practice

Now you're ready to go out and ski some bumps. I've taught many recreational skiers and instructors how to improve their bump skiing using these techniques. Keep in mind the must-have and must-know moves of your mogul repertoire:

- Manage your free foot, bringing it close to the stance foot and drawing it back before you start your turn.
- Have a solid, stabilizing pole plant before the release.

Chapter 13:
Powder

Mysteries of Natural Snow

Ever since I was a child, I knew powder skiing was recognized as the ultimate skiing experience. Unfortunately, it was some time before I actually got my chance to try it. In the years leading up to my first experience, the topic of skiing powder always raised conflicting advice from both instructors and experts. I didn't really know what to expect. My feelings of inadequacy were more than just a passing glitch in confidence; they revolved around my complete lack of practical knowledge and experience on real western snow conditions. My first try in deep powder came in 1968 at Castle Mountain ski area near the Crowsnest Pass, in Alberta, Canada. The heavy wet stuff we used to plow through as kids in the Laurentian Mountains in Eastern Canada was no training ground for that.

Coming from the east coast, I found I was out of my element. The best advice I could garner from my racer buddies was to sit back and twist my skis, and if I got out of control, to lean back and sit down before I ran into a tree. Sound advice for an 18-year-old from an 18-year-old. Advice I received from instructors and other experienced skiers didn't provide much better information. Some said you sat back in powder, others said you hopped. None of the advice made any sense at all to me while I was screaming down through the trees in hip-deep snow. Eventually, I had to admit that my buddy's advice about sitting down to avoid hitting a tree was my most reliable tactic. By the end of the day a combination of guts, close calls and quick reflexes added up to a few connected turns that made me think that there might be something to this powder skiing after all. The rest of that winter I skied all over the west, but mostly in Banff and Lake Louise. I met Mike Wiegele, who was the ski school director in Lake Louise at the time. I skied with everyone I thought could help me and I stuck with Mike whenever I could get him out for some runs. I learned a lot from him, and that experience started my transition to an all-mountain skier.

Most of us don't have the time or the physical capacity to learn to ski powder the way I did, so I have developed a much shorter and safer route.

Looking Good

Powder technique has advanced since those days, although it is not always accompanied by succinct instructions. Ideally, instructions for specific, effective movements are most helpful. You may notice I rely on "how to" movement cues rather than observations or explanations of positions. My coaching experience has taught me that to look good on skis you must be making correct movements. Expert powder skiers look graceful and move effortlessly. Such skiing is attainable by using small movements that create big results, not big movements that require strong muscles.

The snow in this next photo sequence is new powder that has been blown by the wind. In some places it is a foot deep, in others it is only 3 inches over frozen crust. Delicate pressuring was required, especially at the top of the turn. Notice how I describe making the pressure even from ski to ski and flexing both legs to keep them moving laterally as one unit.

Handle the Pressure

Fig. a. Balance with more weight on the outside or downhill ski than on the inside ski to continue turning at the bottom of the arc.

Fig. b. With the pole plant, begin to flex and relax the stance leg. When the stance leg flexes to match the flex of the inside leg, balance on both skis to keep them pressured equally.

Fig. c. Flex your legs and let the skis float until they come to the surface. Keep them at the same edge angles. Use the stabilizing pole plant to balance as the skis surface.

Fig. d. As you flex, press the downhill boot toward the uphill boot and tilt the downhill ski first. Make sure the legs stay pressed together while tilting. Flexing the legs equally and keeping the skis at the same edge angles controls your float.

Fig. e. Do not rush the tipping action - make sure both skis tip together. Flattening the downhill ski and releasing will commit your body to the perfect position for the next turn. PMTS technique lets the body move as a unit into the arc of the new turn, organized and balanced despite the variable snow conditions.

Fig. f. As the skis tip, gradually extend the legs. The edge angle causes the skis to redirect. Then increase the tilt of the inside ski. Notice that the skis changed direction when they were above the snow as a result of tipping the free ski and holding the legs together to work in unison. No active leg rotation or steering is needed.

Fig. g. As the turn comes back far enough in the other direction, begin to flex and release.

Fig. 13-1. Handle the pressure

Biomechanical Advantage

- Both skis will turn together when you keep them at the same edge angles.
- Flexing and tipping to release will move the body into the new turn.

Cues for Success

- Press the entire length of your legs together.
- Stand evenly on both skis during the float.
- Use a stabilizing pole plant.

First Requirement - Mastering the Pressure

Skiing ungroomed snow is a piece of cake if you use the balancing movements you developed from the PMTS Undergraduate Course and trust your skis' side cut to turn. One of the basic skills you should acquire from PMTS is foot awareness and the ability to pressure the skis independently. You can increase or decrease the weight on a ski,or you can transfer balance from one foot to the other. We showed how to develop these abilities in the Undergraduate Course (refer to the float and Weighted Release). In powder, we play with equalizing the pressure on both skis, as well as increasing and decreasing pressure from one ski to the other. Pressuring by extending a leg will sink that ski into the snow; flexing and retracting the leg causes the ski to rise to the surface. When both skis are pressured evenly, you can sustain or increase your buoyancy via the process of quickly flexing or retracting your legs. When we pressure both skis evenly and tip them in the prescribed order, they can behave as one platform. Making the pressure even on the skis is used to develop a release. This technique is described in Chapter 8, "Weighted Release."

Although you try to develop even pressure on both skis coming into the release, in other parts of the turn you still may require different and varied pressure on each ski. You can adjust the pressure with the same movements we have used throughout the PMTS short turn progression, flexing and relaxing the leg to make that ski lighter and extending to create more pressure. In powder, the difference in pressure between the skis becomes more obvious, as the more pressured ski will sink into the snow and the lighter ski will rise to the surface. The emphasis of PMTS Direct Parallel, from the first lesson, has been on shifting balance from one foot to the other. Alternating balance from one ski to the other is stance mastery and is probably the most important prerequisite for skiing off-piste. Reducing the edge grip and the pressure build-up under the skis by the releasing movements starts a new turn in powder, as in all other skiing situations.

This simple warm-up is useful for powder, soft snow or crud snow. The hopping helps to develop and feel a range of motion in the legs. Landing with legs flexed and tipping the inside boot puts the skis on edge and develops a feel for balance as the skis start to engage and turn. Hopping again gives you the opportunity to pressure both skis evenly at take-off. This warm-up also lets you practice the non-stop pole plant needed for powder skiing. To maintain balance, your upper body will need to coordinate with the legs. Revisit the straight run ULEC exercises in Chapter 10 if needed.

Fig. 13-2. Hopping powder warm-up

Fig. a. Start with a straight run. Plant the pole for a direction change to the left.
Fig. b. Hop and tip your skis to the left.
Fig. c. Hold your legs together in the air. Start to swing the basket forward for the next pole plant already.
Fig. d. After you land, tip the inside ski (here, the left) more than the outside ski, but press your legs and boots together.
Fig. e. Flex the legs and settle down on the skis. Let the angle of the skis to the snow create the turn.
Fig. f. Pole plant again and hop. Push evenly off both feet to hop.
Fig. g. Start the next pole swing while you're in the air.
Fig. h. Prepare the new inside ski for tipping and make sure the legs and skis stay together.
Fig. i. Tip the inside ski as you land on the snow, and flex the inside leg further than the outside leg.
Fig. j. Keep minimal pressure on the tipped, inside ski to set the skis into a turn.

Release, Transfer, and Engagement in Powder

In powder, getting into a series of turns from a standing start can be the first and one of the most difficult hurdles. As illustrated in the hopping powder warm-up, *Figure 13-2*, from a straight run begin by extending your legs to push both skis into the snow. You will discover how much resistance the snow has to offer. Once the skis stop sinking you can react. Quickly pop your skis back to the surface by bouncing or flexing, and pulling your knees toward your chest. You can do this 2 or 3 times to pick up a little speed and determine the snow's density. After you have felt the skis reaching the bottom of your extension and know how dense the snow is, plant your pole the next time the skis surface and begin tipping your skis. Try to keep the first turn very short — just enough for a slight direction change. As soon as you tip the skis they will take a set in the snow. A set means the skis are now angled against the directional pull of gravity and pressure will build under the bottoms as they sink. Once the pressure builds sufficiently, the skis will begin deflecting more quickly, causing a turn.

Imagine you are beginning a turn to the left. Keep the inside, left ski pressed against the stance ski boot as they both tip to the inside of the turn. Always initiate tipping by tilting or rolling with the inside ski; let the outside ski and leg follow. Be aware at this point that the inside ski will try to separate from the outside ski. Keep the legs squeezed together in powder to help both skis do the same thing and stay at equal edge angles. As the skis take their set in the soft snow, extend the outside leg. When they stop sinking in the powder, immediately begin to flex the outside leg. Flexing will cause the body to move toward the skis and down the hill. Pull the downhill ski out of the snow as you flex to speed up the transition and transfer your balance to the other ski. Extend the new outside leg and keep tipping and flexing the releasing ski. Now your body is lined up with the new outside ski and you are in balance for the new turn.

The movements of releasing and transfer in powder are the same as in the rest of the book except you may need to be more deliberate with the downhill ski at the end of the turn. You may, in addition to flexing, need to pull the ski out of the snow. In effect this is like kicking one leg out from under a card table. As we all know, the table collapses quickly toward the side of the removed leg. Similarly, the body reacts by falling toward the collapsing, folding, or flexing leg as you remove the support of the old stance leg. The release has begun and is automatically followed by the transfer and engagement. Continue these movements with a stabilizing pole plant and you have the basics of powder and crud skiing.

The first photo sequence of this chapter, *Figure 13-1*, is continued here. Note that it's important not to overload the downhill ski at the bottom of turns in this snow. To come out of powder turns with your shiny side up, flex both legs to release, especially the outside leg, because it will always be longer, or more extended. By flexing it earlier, you have a chance to even out the pressure between the skis. Once the skis are evenly pressured, pull your knees toward your chest to put both skis flat quickly.

Biomechanical Advantage

- When the body moves across the skis to start a turn, keeping the skis at the same edge angle, the snow will deflect the skis together in the turn.

Fig. 13-3. Control the pressure with flexion and extension

Fig. a. Plant the pole and bring both knees up together to get out of the turn.
Fig. b. Hang onto the pole and let the skis float out from under the body. Tip the inside ski.
Fig. c. Lighten the inside ski and tilt it for the new turn.
Fig. d. The releasing and engaging movements of *Figure c* will draw your torso inside both skis. Extend the outside leg to maintain contact with the snow.
Fig. e. Keep the inside ski held close to the stance ski for easier tipping actions. Notice how the inside leg extends with the outside leg.
Fig. f. Strong counteracting movements help to keep you in balance with equally angled skis.
Fig. g. Increase the flex of the inside leg as you tilt that ski to keep pressure equal on the skis and edge angles the same just before the release.

Cues for Success

- To exit the turn, flex both legs, starting with the downhill leg.
- To maintain the turn, continue tipping the inside ski and extending the outside leg.

Make the Skis Behave in Unison

The idea in powder and uneven snow is to make both skis behave like one ski. I imagine a snowboard or a mono-ski. Even as it is tipping, a mono-ski has a more weighted side (the side in the snow) and a less weighted side. But this evens out and reaches a constant state as the wide ski compacts or traps snow under the base surface. As the snow packs under the ski, it begins to feel light and controllable. If you are on two skis, the ski that is completely weighted will sink more deeply, making it difficult to control or turn. Skiing on powder and crud is different from skiing on packed snow, for you are in a more fluid-like medium. Like water skiing, each ski must stay afloat. Quickly overloading or over pressuring one ski relative to the other can make it react unfavorably, probably diving deep and pulling apart from the light ski. Remember, as I said in my first book, "Don't surprise your skis." Independent pressuring of the skis is still necessary in powder, but it must be done in a subtle, more progressive way.

Let's try to create the same effect that gives the mono-ski or snowboard its flotation advantage in soft snow. With the new skis you have, in effect, the opportunity to have a mono-ski on each foot, especially the mid-fats or all-mountain skis. Any ski 70 mm wide under the foot is wide enough to provide great flotation and control in powder or crud, if used correctly. Regulating the pressure from one ski to the other by either flexing or lightening to create float is appropriate. Extending to increase and maintain contact of the outside or stance ski at the beginning of the turn provides momentary balance, but the skis must line up side-by-side at the same edge angle before the turn progresses very far. I will demonstrate how these movements work in different all-mountain conditions in the photo sequences throughout this section. When both skis are lined up before engaging in the new turn, you can maintain consistent turning throughout the arc. During the release, even pressure is beneficial for flotation and is necessary for smooth transitions. The ability to regulate pressure with flexion and extension will allow the skis to behave as one wide platform.

Fig. 13-4. Make the skis behave in unison

There are situations in powder, as shown in this montage, in which the stance or downhill ski gets caught in the snow and does not release as desired. Take the time to organize the releasing ski, lining it up with the new outside ski, before the skis engage.

Fig. a. The turn is almost finished and it's time to get the ski tips out of the snow. Begin to relax the downhill leg.

Fig. b. Flexing the legs will reduce the ski edge angles and will bring your body or torso closer to and over the skis. Try to keep equal pressure on both skis and flex both legs so the skis are lighter on the snow. Let the skis move forward and flatten as you flex.

Fig. c. Synchronize leg flexing and ski flattening with the pole plant to bring the upper body into the next turn. You are controlling your body's entry to the new turn with the angle of the skis. Pull the now lifted and retracted leg and ski in toward the stance ski.

Fig. d. Begin tipping for the next turn. The tipping of the inside ski helps to commit the body into the new turn.

Second Requirement - Keep the Skis at the Same Edge Angle

The ability to keep your feet, skis and boots at exactly the same angles while moving laterally to and from an edge is the second requirement for skiing in soft snow. Here, mastery of the ball control exercise (Chapter 6, *Figure 6-5*) is a must. If you can make your skis and legs tip in unison well enough to ski gentle turns with the ball between your feet, controlling your skis in powder and crud is within your reach. The movement sequence for the release, discussed in the first section of the book, becomes critical when you reach this stage in your skiing. Now in powder and crud you will be able to determine whether you have practiced these techniques sufficiently. The movements of the Undergraduate Course really pay dividends at these upper levels of skiing.

Where Does it Break Down?

Skiers with an A-frame or knock-kneed stance have difficulty keeping the skis at the same edge angle. The A-frame stance is not necessarily a circumstance of poor alignment. It can result from a dominant urge to move the downhill ski to an edge first. Remember, unlike hard pack, powder and crud conditions provide minimal resistance to tipping because they are soft. You easily can tip the new downhill ski too far. I only remind you of this possibility because when you first try to ski in powder you are likely to revert to old habits. This typically stems from an attempt to get the ski turning, on edge, or across the slope. We discussed this in detail in Chapter 4, "Release." However, unless you have properly prepared and applied yourself to learning PMTS Direct Parallel movements, the wrong movement still can return when you are in stressful situations. You are not alone; for most skiers and even for some instructors the tendency is to turn the new downhill ski, especially in powder. This survival instinct is very strong — a default movement pattern that is deeply ingrained. If you still use this default movement, read on and you will learn to change it shortly.

History

In the first section of the book and the early undergraduate chapters, I explained why traditional instruction makes it difficult, if not impossible, to become an expert. Traditional systems rely heavily on commands such as "turn the outside ski," "steer the legs," and "stand on the downhill ski," and are making you work too hard in an incorrect manner. When you apply movements like these to powder or crud snow, you will be in for unpleasant surprises. These traditional movements train you to engage the downhill ski well before the inside ski, thereby putting the skis in a converging relationship, the A-frame. Unfortunately, by the time the inside ski can match the outside ski, the skis are crossed or the downhill ski is overloaded and digs in. Even if you are an inside ski "quick steering sensation," you will get caught crossing your tips from time to time on powder and crud slopes.

Foot Separation

Keep the skis and boots close together or they may act independently. Use the cue of touching the boots to ensure they stay close enough. When your feet are more than an inch apart in soft snow they are more difficult to control. If you don't press the legs together, the skis will pull apart. Once you are in the turn, your skis may separate vertically, but you must keep the inside boot close to the outside leg. If your skis should separate to shoulder width or more in the transition, you quickly will need to pull the free foot back in line, as in *Figure 13-4*. The closer the feet are together, the easier it is to adjust the pressure subtly on each ski. When the boots are together, one movement can control both skis. Remember, the goal is to have two skis behave as one. I like to keep my legs touching so they can react as one unit. In this position, the legs still are able to adjust for up and down, extending and flexing movements. The femurs can still turn under a stable pelvis when your boots are together. If this weren't the case, Jonny Mosely wouldn't be able to survive in the bumps with his locked foot style.

Skis are Rudders

The snow doesn't know whether you have two skis or one wide ski. It responds to what you give it. If you present your skis at two different angles to powder snow, the skis, especially shaped skis, will act as if they each had a mind of their own. Skis in powder are like rudders; they take off in different directions as soon as their angles to the snow differ. They force the boat, or in this case, each leg, to head in different directions. Tipping the wrong ski first pressures it and causes it to react quickly. If you have difficulty now in 4 inches of powder, those movements will only be worsened in 10 inches of snow. This tendency of the skis to separate when tipped at different angles reinforces the idea that shaped skis should not be turned, which is doubly true in powder. Proficient powder skiing can be achieved with simple tipping movements. It's important to remember that in powder, the edges don't have much influence on your turning or holding. The bases (flat, wide, bottom surface) of the skis do. Like the wing of an airplane, the bases are the flat surface area and its exposure to the snow controls direction. Powder skiing requires a different understanding of skiing, but the same PMTS movements can be used successfully.

Ski Action and Reaction

When the skis are tipped at an angle against the direction of travel, the snow gathers under the ski and deflects the skis in a new direction. The idea then is to pack as much snow under the outside ski as under the inside, in order to keep the pressure under both skis the same so that they will change direction together. If you start by tipping the inside ski to the little-toe edge, for example, that ski will deflect and move out of the way, making room for the outside ski to follow. This movement will lean or tilt the body slightly inside the turn, thereby tipping the outside ski appropriately. After that initiating movement of the inside foot, angle both skis equally and they will stay parallel. By tipping the inside ski first, you cause a reaction further up the body that moves your center into the turn. The tilting of your body causes the stance ski to tip on edge passively and thus turn. The outside leg should extend and the inside leg should shorten to keep both skis turning at the same radius through the lower half of the arc.

Fig. 13-5. Keep the skis at the same angle

Fig. a. After the skis have floated, tip the inside ski to the little-toe edge.
Fig. b. Point the pole tip down the hill.
Fig. c. Begin flexing and releasing as you plant the pole.
Fig. d. Flex your legs so that the skis rise to the surface.
Fig. e. Use the stabilizing pole plant for balance.

The ski angles must remain the same if the skis are to act in unison during the turn. After the last turn, the skis were allowed to float and the inside ski was tilted. Keeping both skis together helps keep them under control and facilitates balance adjustments. With the skis working together, very little effort is needed to turn the skis — just small tipping and flexing movements. These movements reduce physical effort and maintain balance. Since you have tipped the skis to make the turn, no body swinging is needed to horse the skis around. Use counteracting movements of the hips to stabilize the torso. Counteracting movements also set up the turn for a powerful release by coiling the upper body against the legs. From *Figures c* to *e* you will notice how the flattening of the skis uncoils the legs. You don't have to concentrate on the legs to achieve this releasing power. Releasing the skis and using the upper and lower body coordination movements we presented in Chapter 10 will produce this effective and efficient way to ski.

Focus on Your Feet to Control the Legs

On intermediate terrain, once you start a turn you have to be prepared to move quickly to turn back in the other direction. You must head back the other way before you go too far across the slope. If you stay in the turn too long, you may lean over and fall to the inside of the turn. Keeping your momentum going down the hill keeps you upright, so use a series of connected turns. Prepare to change direction as soon as you feel the pressure under the skis taking them in the new direction. Change direction by flexing the stance leg, which lightens the stance ski and reduces the pressure on it. Because the stance ski is pressed deeper in the snow throughout the turn, it must be prepared for the transition prior to the inside ski. You may have to flex aggressively to pull it up out of the snow. Flexing the leg will take the pressure off the ski and reduce the snow's influence on it. When the ski starts to flatten, flex both legs equally, and flatten both skis to the snow. When they are both flat on the snow, you will be in between turns and your legs should be bent the most. By flexing your legs, you allow your skis to float and come closer to the surface. When they are near the top, they are easy to tip and redirect into the next turn.

Turning the Skis is Tiring

Many skiers I talk to feel that they need tremendous power to turn the skis in powder. I've seen them grinding away and twisting their legs to change direction. If you feel your muscles starting to burn as you try to overcome the turning resistance, you are working too hard. Turning the skis in powder should be effortless. You shouldn't feel that the skis are hard to turn. We discussed using "the force" in Chapter 7. Releasing the downhill ski allows you to use your momentum and gravity to keep your body moving down the slope rather than trying to stop your momentum with a stiff stance leg and pushing off it to begin a new turn. That's too much work.

If you find yourself working too hard, what's causing this wasted effort? Earlier I described how to extend the stance leg and where to use it in the turn. In powder, most skiers rarely use extension. Instead, they stay in a flexed position. Not only can this be more tiring for the muscles, it doesn't allow any further relaxation of the stance leg to create an effective release. Those skiers hardly ever use "the force." Without a release, the only way to start turns is by jumping and twisting your skis using the larger, leg-turning muscles. These muscles only impart their full twisting power to the skis when they are bent or flexed. If you are trying to turn your skis in powder, you are using these muscles and you have to stay flexed throughout the turn. PMTS saves you from this exhausting and frustrating spiral, but first you must recognize your limiting movements and replace them with efficient PMTS movements.

Flexing and Extending the Legs

In PMTS we advocate flexing the legs but in a completely different way. Flexed legs have turning power, while straight legs have little turning power but are strong for edging. Now you will learn how to use the relationship between turning power and edging power. Imagine making a turn to the left. When your skis flatten after the release, continue tipping the left ski from flat toward its outside or little-toe edge. Allow the right ski to react naturally and keep some tension holding your legs together. The right ski will follow the direction of the left, tipping ski. At the same time, it will have to stretch out or extend to maintain contact with the snow as your body moves inside the turn. Remember, I said "stretch out," not push against the snow. The extension of the right leg on the outside of the turn will tip that ski to an angle in the snow causing the ski to turn toward the fall line. The inside ski leads the tipping activity and should always be angled slightly earlier than the outside ski. The turn has been set into motion. All that is required after this is fine-tuning by making tipping adjustments. As the snow packs under the right ski, it pushes back against the leg, especially as you cross the fall line; the same is true for the inside ski. Keep extending the right leg to pack the snow under the ski until you are ready to start the next turn. The inside leg is more flexed. The body has reacted to the primary movements of tipping the skis. The legs are extended, resulting in strong edging.

For the next turn you must again relax and flex to begin the flattening and tipping of the skis. Here is where flexed legs help to redirect the skis. During transition, the legs follow the flattening and re-engaging of the skis. During edge release, the legs move from uphill of the skis to downhill of the skis. This movement across the skis changes the edge angles and imparts passive steering to the skis. The more flexed the legs are during transition, the more they move across the skis. Thus, flexed legs have greater turning influence on the skis. Remember that you are focused on lateral tipping, not leg turning. Focus on flattening the skis and flexing the legs, and you will achieve the amount of ski redirection you need.

Figure 13-6 shows fresh tracks in wind-packed snow. It is denser than powder, so the skis will react more quickly in it.

Fig. a. The skis are floating, ready for inside ski tilting to increase the body and ski angles to the slope.

Fig. b. Increase inside ski tilting and your body will drop to the inside. Now both skis are angled to the snow. Offering resistance to the snow by extending the legs causes the skis to turn more quickly.

Fig. c. The body is angled to the slope and legs are extended, causing pressure to build under the skis. The skis deflect in the snow to the new direction.

Fig. d. Keep the legs extended until the turn is far enough around to begin releasing. Notice how the pole swing has developed with the wrist movement. Now plant the pole and begin flexing both legs to release and flatten the skis.

Fig. e. Flex both legs and shorten the downhill leg to match the length of uphill leg and pressure of the uphill ski.

Fig. f. Move the downhill leg out of the way by shortening and tipping. This movement will transfer balance and prepare the body to move into the next turn.

Fig. 13-6. Flexion and extension of the legs

Fig. g. Even with strong flexing, crud and wind-blown snow offer strong support and energy to the skis as they are released. I lift out of the snow without jumping or hopping, simply as a result of the skis' planing on the firmly compressed wind pack. Proceed with tipping the inside ski and you will land in perfect balance.

Fig. h. Keep tipping the inside ski to tilt the outside ski on edge. Do not move the outside ski to get it on edge. The edge angle will result from the body's tipping into the turn. Any attempt to put the outside ski on an edge will result in the tail pushing out as well as unequal ski edge angles.

Extending the Outside Leg

The outside leg should be extended to maintain contact and to compress the snow under the ski. You must be judicious with how you extend. Too soon and too much will cause you to push your body down the hill, resulting in loss of balance. The idea is to use the force. Let the tipping action of the inside free foot, momentum and gravity move your body into the next turn. Don't push your body down the hill with your extended outside leg. Tipping the inside ski and flexing the inside leg help to bring the body to the inside of the turn once the transition has begun. As the body moves inside, the outside leg naturally has to extend to stay in contact with the snow, providing an advantage later in the turn when it is time to change direction. An extended outside leg has a large range of flexion and can be used to absorb pressure at the bottom of the turn. When flexion is active and fast, the skis quickly come to the surface and flatten in the process. Keep the upper body facing the same direction during this process of flexing and releasing. Notice from the photos how important the role of the pole plant is to help hold the upper body in position until you are ready for the next turn.

Timing of Linked Turns

Determine when it is time for another turn by how much direction change or turn completion you want. If you are on a very steep powder slope, start flexing the outside leg earlier to slowly control the body's rate of descent into the fall line and the next turn. Don't wait too long or the skis will start into a traverse, carrying your momentum across the hill, no longer available to help with the release. If you have a traverse between turns you will be forced to use the muscle-taxing techniques discussed earlier to initiate the next turn. Timing the flexing and relaxing of the outside leg will dictate your turn size, rhythm and speed. Slow flexing will lengthen the turn; quick, aggressive flexing — almost pulling both legs out of the snow — will create short, quick powder turns.

Retracting the Legs

Retracting the legs or flexing the knees to shorten the legs is a powder power move that often is needed for skiing in very steep powder runs. Many skiers have difficulty practicing this move because they rarely want to learn by experimenting in challenging conditions. Practice the retraction and flexing movements demonstrated in Chapter 7 in your regular short turns and you will become familiar with the movements.

PMTS movements develop an extended outside leg near the middle of the turn. This extension of the leg offers a complete range of flexion. Near the end of the turn, it is important to use this range of flexion to get out of the turn. If you quickly retract and flex your leg, you are taking the pressure off your ski. The ski, therefore, floats to the top of the snow. Hold this float position for a moment until you are sure that both skis are at the same angle and you are in balance. Now, with both legs flexed, you can begin tipping the outside or lower ski toward the outside edge to begin the transition. In powder, relaxing and flexing the legs to end a turn has a greater impact than on groomed snow. As the flexing brings your skis flat and up to the snow surface, you are ready to begin tipping. Once your legs are flexed sufficiently and you have placed your pole, you are ready to let the skis float.

Fig. 13-7. Retract the legs for a clean release in crud

Fig. a. Strong flexion and retraction (pulling up on the legs) allow my skis to float over this crud.
Fig. b. Strong, quick inside ski tipping engages the skis.
Fig. c. Short turns in this crud again require strong flexing.
Fig. d. Flex the legs and pull the knees up when the snow is sticky.
Fig. e. When the skis are free from the snow, tip in the new direction.
Fig. f. When the legs are strongly flexed, as in this sequence, tipping has an instant turning effect. As at the top of a bump, a large direction change can be made by tipping the flexed legs.

Dryland Training for Leg Flexion and Extension

Quickly flexing and retracting the leg is not a natural movement. One of the best ways to practice strong flexing and retracting actions without powder, or even lift lines, is the dryland skiing machine called the Skier's Edge. If you are having trouble performing the leg retraction and flexing movements described here, try the Skier's Edge. It duplicates the extension and absorption movements in your own living room, and, if you set up a mirror, you can watch yourself to ensure your legs flex and extend. The machine also allows your feet to tip and reproduce the controlling movements that keep the skis at the same edge angles. If used correctly, it duplicates the movements of PMTS.

Pole Plant and Arm Rhythm

There is no substitute for good hand and pole use in powder skiing. All the principles demonstrated in Chapter 10, or in the *PMTS Instructor Manual*, will help you develop strong pole use in powder. The arms and poles shouldn't be conducting an orchestra in any kind of skiing, unless you are in trouble and need a gross reaction to recover. The arms and poles can't create a release, but they can time movements and stabilize the upper body. No amount of arm reaching or swinging will start a turn unless you release the skis. Early preparation for the turn by pointing the pole tip down the fall line is a great way to keep the body in line and prepared for the eventuality of the ski's release. Proper arm and pole use will keep the upper body in position and efficiently balanced. After the pole is planted in the snow, punch the inside hand forward to keep from over-rotating the upper body. Often, in the excitement of a steep powder run, this movement is forgotten. The hand and arm are dragged back by the pole plant, the body swings around to face the side of the trail, and you overturn. I recommend you practice continuous arm movements in your warm-up runs to establish the proper poling activity. Prepare your pole early for the turn. Pull your hand toward your shoulder so you can swing the tip of the pole and point it down the slope before planting it into the snow. This movement will assure proper shoulder and arm positioning prior to the turn, just as I explained in the sections on pole use (Chapter 10).

Steep Powder

After riding powerful motorcycles, jumping out of an airplane, and racing on a World Cup downhill course, I still believe steep powder runs are the most exhilarating feeling in sports. They're not only exciting, but you'll find that steep powder runs can be very safe if you are in the right place at the right time. The ideal powder for this experience is dry. Wet powder slows you down too much and requires very steep slopes where cliffs and rocks often become hazards. My best experiences with steep powder were at Snowbird, Alta, Berthoud Pass and the Canadian Bugaboos and Monashees. I am sure other powder experiences exist, but for easy access, Loveland and Berthoud Pass in Colorado, and Snowbird in Utah, are the most readily accessible. You must be crafty to take advantage of the powder at Snowbird these days, because the local population knows how to use up the untracked snow in short order. One option is to take a guess on the weather or a storm pattern. Stay overnight up in the canyon before they close the road and have the mountain to yourself the next day, for no one can get up the canyon when it is snowed in. For me the best is Berthoud Pass, about a half-hour from my house; I get a big jump on the Denver traffic even on a weekend day. Once you have found that steep section you want with no tracks and no one around, don't hesitate. The next skier may not stop to look around and check the view. He will most likely just ski right past your perch and poach your run. You may have heard the saying, "No friends on a powder day." Remember though, before you take on something new, it is best to know the area you are about to ski. You never know what is beyond the next tree or steep drop.

Free Falling

You are ready, you push off, but the first turn seems heavy and the skis don't respond. Powder skiing requires momentum just like carving high-angle turns. Let your skis go at first and make less direction change. Definitely keep your poles moving, and make strong continuous pole plants. In powder, never stop moving your hands and wrists. You must prepare constantly for the next turn with an early pole plant. At this point, many skiers try to slow themselves down by making sharper turns before they reach cruising velocity. You may be holding yourself back from experiencing the most thrilling ride of your life by bailing out too early. Even on very steep slopes, the powder should be enough to slow you down; try not to use sharp turns to control speed. If you do, your skis will dig in and you won't be floating over the surface; you'll be on the ground. The real experience of flying in powder means that you shouldn't touch the packed snow beneath the new. The flying sensation comes from staying above the hard surface and well up in the new snow. Speed control isn't the issue; you eventually will reach maximum velocity and stay at that speed for the rest of the run. Snow density and deepness determine maximum speed. Turns can help to reduce speed, but not to control it. Most important, as I said earlier, know the slope and the run-out area. Free falling on skis is not for everyone, but if you are ready to experience this thrill, make sure you have more than 6 inches of new snow. In fact, you really need at least a foot and a half to two feet to experience this type of skiing.

Trees

Skiing powder in the trees is simple if you have mastered the basic technique. Figure it out on open terrain first. In the trees is where you should use the fat powder skis. In open snowfields, regular-waisted shaped skis are fine because you can use speed to keep them floating. In the trees, you may not want to have as much speed as you need to keep such skis above the snow. In fact, this happened to me on a cat powder skiing tour at Steamboat. I could ski the steep powder on my longish skis when I was in the open. But when the aspen trees were close together, I often missed great skiing lines because my skis would bog down in the tight turns dictated by the trees. I immediately switched to wide, shaped powder skis and the world changed. All of a sudden I could keep a rhythm going, make the turns around the trees, and still stay on top of the snow.

Trees can be intimidating and they should command your respect. Using them as slalom poles is not a good idea. Kim Reichhelm, the former world extreme champion, once used a large pine for a GS pole while filming for a Warren Miller movie and found it wasn't forgiving. She tore her shoulder and went bouncing down the slope. Tactics for tree skiing are similar to those you use in mountain biking. Never look at the trees! Always look for the light between the trees. Give yourself more than 3 feet from the edge of the tree well (the hole around the tree trunk) because your body has to be angled toward the tree to make the turn. If you have to sneak by trees that are close together, move your upper body outward over the stance ski. Some of the best snow ever found is in the trees, but there are also obstacles such as fallen logs and thinly covered rocks. I suggest you wait until they have all been covered by a number of big snowstorms before you get started.

References

Bacharach, D., Seifert, J., Dean, K., Shultz, D., and Rice, L., (2000). *Coaching Cues via Radio Enhance Practice Performance of Junior Alpine Skiers. Abstracts,* 2nd International Congress on Skiing and Science.

Harb, Harald (1997). *Anyone can be an Expert Skier*. New York: Hatherleigh Press.

Harb, H., Rogers, D., Hintermeister, R., and Peterson, K., (1998). *Primary Movements Teaching System Instructor Manual*. Colorado: Harb Ski Systems.

Harb, H. and Frediani, P., (2001). *Ski Flex*. New York: Hatherleigh Press.

Tejada-Flores, Lito (1986). *Breakthrough on Skis*. New York: Vintage Books.

Wulf, G. and Wiegelt, C., (1997). Instructions about physical principles in learning a complex motor skill: To tell or not to tell… *Res. Qtrly. For Exer. & Sport, 68*, 362-367.

Wulf, G., Hoss, M., and Prinz, W., (1998). Instructions for motor learning: Differential effects of internal versus external focus of attention. *J. Mot. Behav., 30*, 169-179.

Anyone Can Be An Expert Skier 1
The New Way to Ski

Harald Harb enthusiastically offers a step-by-step, easy-to-follow process that will improve your skiing no matter what your ability level. With Harb's revolutionary PMTS Direct Parallel method, you will be on the fast track to all-mountain expert skiing! What's more, you'll learn to recognize, correct and avoid the dead-end movements that keep you from achieving your skiing potential.

Easy-to-understand and impressively complete, this book is a "must have" for skiers everywhere. Quite simply, it is regarded as the foremost authoritative guide to the art of carving with shaped skis.

Anyone Can Be An Expert Skier 1–
The New Way to Ski
Book (ISBN 1-57826-073-6) $19.95
Video (ISBN 1-57826-082-5) $24.95

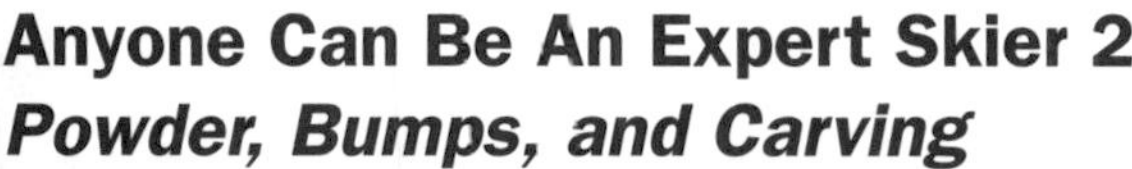

Anyone Can Be An Expert Skier 2
Powder, Bumps, and Carving

Revealed here for the first time: the secrets of the Biomechanical Advantage–a proven technique used by hundreds of pro skiers to achieve winning performance!

In this book and video, you'll learn how to handle challenging terrains and conditions with ease. Moguls, powder and crud, steeps–there will be no limit to your skiing horizons! The special section on advanced carving techniques will perfect your skiing style–giving you precision and control like never before.

Anyone Can Be An Expert Skier 2 is your ideal solution for all mountain conditions. You will discover the techniques that have helped thousands of skiers reach the pinnacle of expert status. Guaranteed!

Anyone Can Be An Expert Skier 2–
Powder, Bumps, and Carving
Book (ISBN 1-57826-074-4) $19.95
Video (ISBN 1-57826-083-3) $24.95

ORDER TOLL FREE 1-800-906-1234

About the Author

Harald Harb, skiing innovator, pioneer of ski instruction, and president of Harb Ski Systems, has made a life-long study of skiing techniques. Born in Austria, he raced the World Cup circuit with the Canadian National Ski Team and later was named Overall Champion on the Eastern US Regional Pro Circuit. As a coach, Harald directed ski racing programs that produced some of the United States' most successful National Team members and Olympic medalists. After working with recreational skiers, he became convinced that current teaching systems needed improvement, so he created the Primary Movements Teaching System (PMTS). Harb also reaches thousands of ski enthusiasts through his position as technical editor at *Skiing* magazine.

Ski with Harald Harb

Here's your chance to ski with Harald Harb and his hand-selected and personally trained staff.

This is a ski experience you will never forget—it could change your skiing for life. Harald Harb and Diana Rogers are the authors and producers of the Anyone Can Be An Expert Skier book and video series. Their company, Harb Ski Systems, offers camps and individual lessons using the techniques described in their books and videos for skiers of all levels and abilities.

Harald invented the PMTS Direct Parallel® system, which has caught the imagination of skiers and ski instructors all over the USA. Harald is also a pioneer in the art of alignment, foot bed design, and boot fitting. All Harb Ski Systems' Green/Blue and Blue/Dark Blue camps include indoor and on-snow alignment evaluations. The All-Mountain and Race camps include an on-snow evaluation; while indoor evaluations can be scheduled individually outside of camp hours.

For more information about the Harb Ski Systems camps—including enrollment details, schedules, and prices—visit the Harb Ski Systems Web site: www.harbskisystems.com or call 303-567-4663.

1. Manage your Free Foot

• Touch the inside boot to the stance boot.

• Keep the boots even fore/aft.

3. The Phantom Move

• Touch the outside edge of the inside ski tip to the snow, and hold the tail a few inches above the snow.

• Touch the free boot to the inside ankle of the stance boot.

5. "Ball Control"

• Squeeze the ball with the free boot against the stance boot.

• Deliberately flatten your stance ski to release.

7. Weighted Release

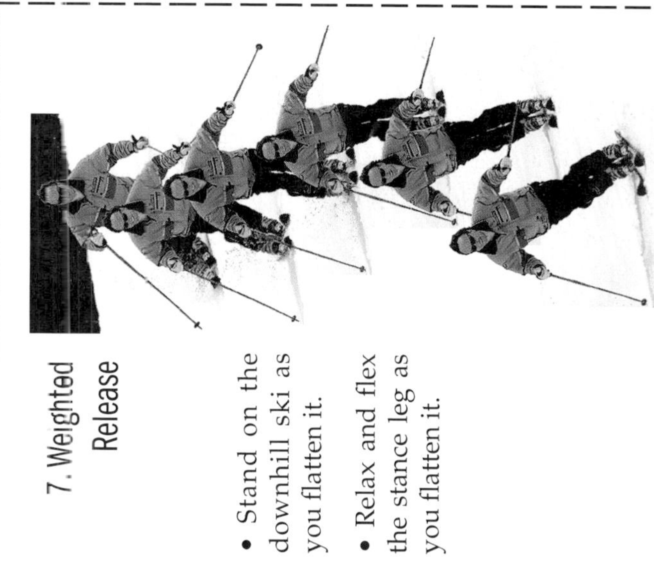

• Stand on the downhill ski as you flatten it.

• Relax and flex the stance leg as you flatten it.

9. Pole/Arch Lift

• Lift inside hand, arm, and shoulder.

• Lift the arch and arm together.

11. Carving in the Bumps

• At the top of the bump, lift the downhill ski, pull it in and back, and tip it over to the outside edge.

• Use a stabilizing pole plant, and the strong inside arm position.

4. Release from the Uphill Edge

- Balance on the little-toe edge of the uphill ski.
- Press the lifted boot against the stance boot throughout the complete turn.
- Flatten the stance ski slowly.

2. Pole Press with Partner

- With the free boot touching the stance boot, have your partner push your foot away while you press inward to maintain contact between the boots.

8. Float in Transition

- Relax, then actively flex the legs to release.
- Pause in tipping the free foot while the skis are flat on the snow surface.

6. Flex to Release

- Pull your knees up toward your chest to achieve leg flexion.
- Pull your free foot in and back to maintain contact with the stance foot.

12. Retract for a Clean Release in Crud

- Flex the legs and pull the knees up toward the chest.
- When the skis are free from the snow, tip the inside ski quickly.

10. Tighten the Carved Arc

- Slide the inside foot up along the outside leg to pull your body into the turn.
- Tip the inside ski onto its outside edge far enough that the inside thigh moves outward.